Epistle to the Church in America: Something Needs to Be Said

Troy Lee Shaw, Ph.D.

Epistle to the Church in America:

Something Needs to Be Said

ISBN-13: 978-0615530918
Library of Congress Control Number: 2011937878
Copyright © August 2011
By Troy Lee Shaw, Ph.D.
First Edition

Patmos Isle Publishing
www.patmosmedia.com

The Cover

Fragmented Dead Sea Psalms Scroll of Qumran Cave 11

בי לוא רמה תידה לכה ולוא תספר חסדכה תולעה

חי חי   יודה לכה יודו לכה כול סוטטי רגל בהודיעכה

חסדכה להמה וצידקתכה תעכילום בי בידכה נפש כול

חי נשמת כול   בשר אתה נתתה עשה עמנו יגיגיא

כטובכה כרוב רחמיכה וכרוב צדקותיכה שבע

יגיגיא בקול אדרובי שמו ולוא עזב חסדו מהבה

בידך יגיגיא עושה צדיקות מעטר חסידיו

חסד ורחמים שאגה נפשי להלל שמכה להודית בינה

הסדיכה ליגיד אמונתכה לתהלתכה אין חקר למות

הייתי בחטאי ועוונתי לשאול מכירוני ותצילני

יגיגיא כרוב רחמיכה וכרוב צדקותיכה גם אני את

שמכה ארבתי ובצלכה חסיתי בזוכרי עוזכה יתקף

לבי ועל חסדיכה אני נסמכתי סלחה יגיגיא לחטאתי

וטהרני מעווני רוח אמונה ורעת חנני אל אתקלה

בעוויה אל ישלט בי שטן ורוח טמאה מכאוב וצר

רע אל ירש בעצמי כי אתה יגיגיא שבחי ולכה קוותי

כיל היום ישמחו אחי עמי ובית אבי השוממים בחונכה

ולם אשמחה בכה

Plea for Deliverance (A Non-canonical Psalm)

Surely a maggot cannot praise thee nor a grave worm recount thy loving-kindness. But the living can praise thee, even those who stumble can laud thee. In revealing thy kindness to them and by thy righteousness thou dost enlighten them. For in thy hand is the soul of every living thing; the breath of all flesh hast thou given. Deal with us, O LORD, according to thy goodness, according to thy great mercy, and according to thy many righteous deeds. The LORD has heeded the voice of those who love his name and has not deprived them of his loving-kindness. Blessed be the LORD, who executes righteous deeds, crowning his saints with loving-kindness and mercy. My soul cries out to praise thy name, to sing high praises for thy loving deeds, to proclaim thy faithfulness- -of praise of thee there is no end. Near death was I for my sins, and my iniquities have sold me to the grave; but thou didst save me, O LORD, according to thy great mercy, and according to thy many righteous deeds. Indeed have I loved thy name, and in thy protection have I found refuge. When I remember thy might my heart is brave, and upon thy mercies do I lean. Forgive my sin, O LORD, and purify me from my iniquity. Vouchsafe me a spirit of faith and knowledge, and let me not be dishonored in ruin. Let not Satan rule over me, nor an unclean spirit; neither let pain nor the evil inclination take possession of my bones. For thou, O LORD, art my praise, and in thee do I hope all the day. Let my brothers rejoice with me and the house of my father, who are astonished by thy graciousness. For ever I will rejoice in thee.

DEDICATION

I dedicate this work to my Grandmother (Margie) - she taught me to respect and tell the truth.

Last but certainly not least, all gratitude, glorification, and plaudit be to God and the ancestors whose past, presence, and power leads us through the state of ever being.

Contents

Epistle to the Church in America: Something Needs to Be Said

INTRODUCTION
Reason for Writing to American Churches

I grew up in the Midwest in a moderate Christian family. We traveled throughout the United States to attend Christian conferences, gilded with people from a variety of denominations. I have been connected to the church all of my life and many stories have emerged from relationships with church goers across the country. Unfortunately, people tend to talk about the negative aspects of church more than the positive attributes; yet it seems odd that the many people captured by negative gossip have been members of a church for years. It seems strange to me that dissatisfied people will remain in a church, even though they dislike a great number of things

1

about the pastor and/or congregation. Frequently congregations are destroyed by negative talking people who are undernourished spiritually.

When a church fails to teach the way of Christ, it diminishes the capacity for healthy growth. We must have more than bodies filling seats – as a matter of fact it seems that a church full of negative nonreciprocal congregants are more often a liability and not an asset. Dissatisfied people are merely journalists coming to a press conference, seeking more negative stories to tell about the church; they contribute little to the true success of the church – and it costs us more to house them than it is worth. Now, it is fully understandable that we live with divine hope as we seek the salvation of all; so we tell ourselves that as long as these mean irritated people come to church, there is a chance that they might someday experience God and become converted. That dream would be great if we were not afraid of losing the crowd, which causes us to often cater to the crows – and because we live in an American social construction, it seems that pluralistic democracy becomes the governing reality of the church. Far too often we look to democratic demons, delegating diplomatic disciples to govern the church; and we end up neglecting ministry to focus on the marginally mundane modicums of meaningless ministry – with the overarching ideology that the people have the answer; when in fact they cannot possibly have the answer without the wisdom of God through the life of Christ, empowered by the movement of the Holy Spirit.

Many of our churches are within a state of decline; even with the field's new crop of multiplexed church systems – attendance is down and declining. The viability, value, and vitality of the church seems to be slipping away as we struggle to hold the pieces together through weekly entertainment experiences; hoping that the godlike glitz will capture season ticket holders. It seems that the church is experimenting and hoping that everything will come out right without inviting the way of Christ into the ministry, mission, and movement of the church.

This epistle is a collection of my thoughts toward the church. The writings may seem extremely unorganized and at times the conversation may ramble – some thoughts may even be incomplete, left for you to work on, or maybe I'll pick them up later. There may be times when my thoughts contradict themselves, don't worry about it – I'm not applying for the position of God. Hopefully, you will read this work as if you were walking through a used shop or flea market; picking through things that you can use and making note of the stuff you left behind. The chapters/articles are not in any specific canonical order – start in the back, front, or middle. This is not an academically motivated dissertation, hoping for the approval of advisors or anybody else – this is just real talk that you are welcome to say amen or disagree.

Nevertheless, I pray that something will be useful as you continue the journey.

The Father, The Son, and Who Else?
The Holy Spirit is our contemporary God form

> *John 14:25-26 These things have I spoken unto you, being yet present with you. But the Comforter, which is the Holy Ghost, whom the Father will send in my name, he shall teach you all things, and bring all things to your remembrance, whatsoever I have said unto you.*

We know God the Father and the Son, and sermon after sermon seems to focus on the Father or the Son but the Holy Spirit is often marginalized as a mere spirit of worship that conducts good entertainment. Unfortunately there are a great number of pastors and Christians who are unfamiliar with the Holy Spirit and the great contemporary work that could emerge within the church if the ever-present Holy Spirit were embraced with active awareness.

I've notice an increasing number of sermons and books on grace, which often turns into an exposition on how to obtain a license to sin. The personal desire to keep people happy often parades us to a place whereby we instantly paint God as completely grace-filled, when we fail to find ways to affirm sin within the scriptures. We ignore the voice of the Holy Spirit, as many of us preach sermons that confirm but never convict. There are times when no is an appropriate word, even though we live in a culture that seeks not to use no – just offer another choice. The church cannot always offer another choice, and there should never be an alternative to the scriptures. The Holy Spirit is our guide. The church must seek the present person of God, just as the Israelites sought God the Father and the people of the Gospels sought Christ.

The Holy Spirit is not just for Sunday worship

John 16:12-14 I have yet many things to say unto you, but ye cannot bear them now. Howbeit when he, the Spirit of truth, is come, he will guide you into all truth: for he shall not speak of himself; but whatsoever he shall hear, that shall he speak: and he will shew you things to come. He shall glorify me: for he shall receive of mine, and shall shew it unto you.

Our lives would be greatly enriched if we would embrace the Holy Spirit as more than a production manager for Sunday worship. I honestly believe that one of the reasons a great number of misinterpreted scriptures are becoming normative evolutions stems from the fact that we have shut out the present person of God charged with leading us into truth and accurate interpretive applications. The Holy Spirit will lead us in holiness, sanctification, and in all matters of life if we are receptive.

8

Matthew 12:32 And whosoever speaketh a word against the Son of man, it shall be forgiven him: but whosoever speaketh against the Holy Ghost, it shall not be forgiven him, neither in this world, neither in the world to come.

Christ taught that we could not be forgiven for blasphemy against the Holy Spirit – which should lead us to understand the importance of our relationship with the Spirit.

The Holy Spirit should be present with each of us on a daily basis – leading us to live while embracing the scriptures. The Holy Spirit presents the proper perspective to live in conjunction with God's truth as applied to our lives.

God has always had the power to heal. As God the Father told the Israelites the conditions for healing (2 Chronicles 7:14), God the Son healed a great number of people and we are prominently healed by His stripes (1Peter 2:24). Although we embrace the historical accounts of God's work it seems that we lack expectancy with regards to the Holy Spirit. Although the Israelites did not do everything right they still knew to seek the Father when in trouble. Even though there were people against the Son, there were a great number of people seeking Him. When the history of the modern movement of God's people is articulated – it seems that there will be a sad dissertation on our lack of desire to be in the true presence of the Holy Spirit. The church within this generation should be just as excited with regards to the Holy Spirit; as the multitudes were when they heard Christ was near.

The Holy Spirit is for everyone

Joel 2:28-29 And it shall come to pass afterward, that I will pour out my spirit upon all flesh; and your sons and your daughters shall prophesy, your old men shall dream dreams, your young men shall see visions: And also upon the servants and upon the handmaids in those days will I pour out my spirit.

Acts 2:16-18 But this is that which was spoken by the prophet Joel; And it shall come to pass in the last days, saith God, I will pour out of my Spirit upon all flesh: and your sons and your daughters shall prophesy, and your young men shall see visions, and your old men shall dream dreams: And on my servants and on my handmaidens I will pour out in those days of my Spirit; and they shall prophesy:

The biggest difference between the three personalities of God is that the Father concentrated on the chosen of

Israel, the Son came to redeem His own, but the Spirit is present to clothe all. All are welcome, yet the truth must be presented through the guidance of the Holy Spirit. If we don't allow the Spirit to have the proper place within the church we are standing in the way of the great movement that the Lord will have upon not some, but all flesh. The young, old, rich, poor, female, and male have the opportunity to receive of God through the personality of the Holy Spirit. Let all come, let all stay, let the Holy Spirit do the rest.

The enemy wants us to continually affix our thinking upon a limited Sunday made for worship Holy Spirit, when instead we must become challenged to magnify the Holy Spirit in all aspects of life.

Mama don't preach

In some churches women are still separated from ministry, and discriminatorily prohibited from serving as a minister and/or deacon.

The Mary factor

God created man first and then woman, therefore it seems only natural that the order of all things would follow this paradigm. Mankind was given charge through Abraham to spiritually influence the families of the world. God connected with man first.

> *Genesis 12:1-3 Now the LORD had said unto Abram, Get thee out of thy country, and from thy kindred, and from thy father's house, unto a land that I will shew thee: And I will make of thee a great nation, and I will bless thee, and make thy name great; and thou shalt be a blessing:* ***And I will bless them that bless thee, and curse him that curseth thee: and in thee shall all families of the earth be blessed.***

13

The Old Testament is the articulation of man's struggle to live within the covenant; however, man continued to disobey God. Genesis begins with man, and woman comes from man. The New Testament begins with Matthew's account of salvation born through the vessel of a woman.

Matthew 1:18-25 **The birth of Jesus Christ came about this way: After His mother Mary had been engaged to Joseph, before they came together, she was found to be with child by the Holy Spirit.** *So Joseph, her husband, being a righteous man, and not wanting to disgrace her publicly, decided to divorce her secretly. But after he had considered these things, an angel of the Lord suddenly appeared to him in a dream, saying, "Joseph, son of David, don't be afraid to take Mary as your wife, because what has been conceived in her is by the Holy Spirit. She will give birth to a son, and you are to name Him Jesus,* *because He will save His people from their sins." Now all this took place to fulfill what was spoken by the Lord through the prophet: See, the virgin will be with child and give birth to a son, and they will name Him Emmanuel, which is translated "God is with us." When Joseph woke up from his sleep, he did as the Lord's angel had commanded him. He took his wife home, but he did not know her intimately until she gave birth to a son. And he named Him Jesus.*

It seems that the issue of whether women can or cannot preach, is one of power – does God have the power to use any vessel or does the Gospel become void when articulated by a woman? The first Adam was formed, the second was born without the primary use of man. Mary the Mother of Christ was in fact God's first vessel within the context of the New Testament; she released the "word," visibly manifested within flesh.

Preacher, pew, and polity

The Apostle Paul provides several doctrinal codexes that at times seem codicillary. Paul is afforded the divine right to create certain doctrinal policies – authority bestowed by Christ through his edict to the disciples. Essentially an Apostle has the authority to bind certain things on earth and they become bound in heaven – creating a system of policies, commonly known as dogma.

Dogma

The word dogma (Gr. *dogma* from *dokein*) signifies, in the writings of the ancient classical authors, sometimes, an opinion or that which seems true to a person; sometimes, the philosophical doctrines[1] or tenets, and especially the distinctive philosophical doctrines, of a particular school of philosophers (Acts 2:9), and sometimes, a public decree or ordinance, as

---

[1] Commonly and definitively interchangeable.

dogma poieisthai. In Sacred Scripture it is used, at one time, in the sense of a decree or edict of the civil authority, as in Luke2:1 "And it came to pass, that in those days there went out a decree [edictum, *dogma*] from Caesar Augustus" (Acts, 17:7, Esther 3:3); at another time, in the sense of an ordinance of the Mosaic Law as in Ephesians 2:15: "Making void the law of commandments contained in decrees" (*dogmasin*[2]), and again, it is applied to the ordinances or decrees of the first Apostolic Council in Jerusalem: "And as they passed through the cities, they delivered unto them the decrees [*dogmata*] for to keep, that were decreed by the apostles and ancients who were at Jerusalem" (Acts 16:4). Among the early Fathers the usage was prevalent of designating as dogmas the doctrines and moral precepts taught or promulgated by the Saviour or by the

---

[2] Meaning: sin against dogma

17

Apostles; and a distinction was sometimes made between Divine, Apostolic, and Ecclesiastical dogmas, according as a doctrine was conceived as having been taught by Christ, by the Apostles, or as having been delivered to the faithful by the Church.[3]

Matthew 16:13-20 When Jesus came into the coasts of Caesarea Philippi, he asked his disciples, saying, Whom do men say that I the Son of man am? And they said, Some say that thou art John the Baptist: some, Elias; and others, Jeremias, or one of the prophets. He saith unto them, But whom say ye that I am? And Simon Peter answered and said, Thou art the Christ, the Son of the living God. And Jesus answered and said unto him, Blessed art thou, Simon Barjona: for flesh and blood hath not revealed it unto thee, but my Father which is in heaven. And I say also unto thee, That thou art Peter, and upon this rock I will build my

[3] The Catholic Encyclopedia, Volume V Copyright © 1909 by Robert Appleton Company Online Edition Copyright © 1999 by Kevin Knight Nihil Obstat, May 1, 1909. Remy Lafort, Censor Imprimatur. +John M. Farley, Archbishop of New York

church; and the gates of hell shall not prevail against it. And I will give unto thee the keys of the kingdom of heaven: and whatsoever thou shalt bind on earth shall be bound in heaven: and whatsoever thou shalt loose on earth shall be loosed in heaven. Then charged he his disciples that they should tell no man that he was Jesus the Christ.

Within the church and organized religion there are countless policies that are created with assertive inference that the doctrine requires adjustment for the overall good of general operations (i.e., decency and order I Cor. 14:40). Clergy continue to embrace the right to influence church polity, as Paul did within the early church history. Paul eradicated gender issues as he wrote to the churches in Galatia – as he proclaimed that there is neither male or female in Christ. Certainly women are welcome within all forms of ministry if the issue of gender becomes *nulls dokein.*

Galatians 3:27 For as many of you as have been baptized into Christ have put on Christ. **There is neither Jew nor Greek, there is neither bond nor free, there is neither male nor female: for ye are all one in Christ Jesus.** *And if ye be Christ's, then are ye Abraham's seed, and heirs according to the promise.*

Although Paul levels the issue of gender within the churches at Galatia, he wrote to Timothy and the Corinthian church – and proclaimed that it is a shame for a woman to speak.

> *1 Corinthians 14:34-35 Let your women keep silence in the churches: for it is not permitted unto them to speak; but they are commanded to be under obedience, as also saith the law. And if they will learn any thing,* **let** *them ask their husbands at home: for it is a shame for women to speak in the church.*

20

*1 Timothy 2:9-15 In like manner also, that women adorn themselves in modest apparel, with shamefacedness and sobriety; not with broided hair, or gold, or pearls, or costly array; But (which becometh women professing godliness) with good works. Let the woman learn in silence with all subjection. **But I suffer not a woman to teach, nor to usurp authority over the man, but to be in silence.** For Adam was first formed, then Eve. And Adam was not deceived, but the woman being deceived was in the transgression. Notwithstanding she shall be saved in childbearing, if they continue in faith and charity and holiness with sobriety.*

These scriptures are often used in terms of restraining women from ministry. However there are several problematic issues. We must notice that within his letter to Timothy, Paul continually says; "I," (1 Timothy 2:12)

21

therefore it does not seem plausible to adopt his statement as a universal law. Furthermore, The King James Version of the Bible uses the term "let" not "make," within the Corinthian text. Upon further analysis we could choose to acquire etymological clarity through the Greek lexicons, however, this would not necessary provide any additional aid for two reasons.

1. Language is primarily understood through the context of culture; we do not live within the culture of the original Greek language – therefore all of our linguistically enlightened etymological studies can only produce a limited understanding of the truth and we are subject to transliterate the translation.

2. It seems clear that Paul is writing to specific issues within the congregations that he was given charge over – as an Apostle. Finally, we will continue to have some churches that will follow certain doctrines given

through the divine insight of a particular leader and movement - and yet localized policy does not automatically become universal law.

To be or not to be

Within Christianity it is commonly conceived that a believer must follow Christ, and the ultimate goal is to become like Christ in every way - as a matter of fact, Christ said that we will do greater works (John 14:12).

> *John 10:22-38 And it was at Jerusalem the feast of the dedication, and it was winter. And Jesus walked in the temple in Solomon's porch. Then came the Jews round about him, and said unto him, How long dost thou make us to doubt? If thou be the Christ, tell us plainly. Jesus answered them, I told you, and ye believed not: the works that I do in my Father's name, they bear witness*

of me. But ye believe not, because ye are not of my sheep, as I said unto you. **My sheep hear my voice, and I know them, and they follow me:** *And I give unto them eternal life; and they shall never perish, neither shall any man pluck them out of my hand. My Father, which gave them me, is greater than all; and no man is able to pluck them out of my Father's hand. I and my Father are one. Then the Jews took up stones again to stone him.*

Centuries have passed and preachers seem to continually advocate that people become like Christ, yet if a woman cannot enter into all forms of ministry – then she cannot ultimately become fully like Christ. At what point should our women stop following Christ? Are we commissioned to restrain our wives, mothers, and daughters from becoming like Christ? If the word ever gets out that women do not have to become fully like

Christ – the world would break out in massive waves of sin! I don't want my daughters to emulate Jezebel – I would think they should be like Christ. When Christ spoke of the children, he did not separate them by gender. Christ admonished us to become like the children – and kids don't normally posses the psychological development to differentiate gender roles.

> *Matthew 19:13-15 Then were there brought unto him little children, that he should put his hands on them, and pray: and the disciples rebuked them.* **But Jesus said, Suffer little children, and forbid them not, to come unto me: for of such is the kingdom of heaven.** *And he laid his hands on them, and departed thence.*

Even with man leading woman, the ultimate end leads to the work of Christ which includes all forms of ministry.

1 Corinthians 11:1-16 Be ye followers of me, even as I also am of Christ. Now I praise you, brethren, that ye remember me in all things, and keep the ordinances, as I delivered them to you. **But I would have you know, that the head of every man is Christ; and the head of the woman is the man; and the head of Christ is God.**

When a woman follows her husband, as he follows Christ (Ephesians 5:21-33) ultimately both of them have the capacity to take on any call of God. Unless we believe that God can not call a woman, and we should know that God is supreme with ways high above our ways; therefore we must embrace women in all dimensions of ministry. God made an ass (female) to speak:

Numbers 22:28-31 **And** *the LORD opened the mouth of the ass, and* <u>she</u> *said* **unto Balaam, What have I done unto thee, that thou hast smitten me these three times?** *And* **Balaam said unto the ass, Because thou hast mocked me: I would there were a sword in mine hand, for now would I kill thee. And the ass said unto Balaam, Am not I thine ass, upon which thou hast ridden ever since I was thine unto this day? Was I ever wont to do so unto thee? And he said, Nay. Then the LORD opened the eyes of Balaam, and he saw the angel of the LORD standing in the way, and his sword drawn in his hand: and he bowed down his head, and fell flat on his face.**

Our tradition is not God's tradition, we have not witnessed all that God can and/or will do. When the work of Christ is done, should we stop the work to satisfy our egos? The scriptures seem to admonish us to allow the work of Christ to continue in spite of our proclivity toward mundane mandates and temporal traditions.

> *Mark 9:30-40 And they departed thence, and passed through Galilee; and he would not that any man should know it. For he taught his disciples, and said unto them, The Son of man is delivered into the hands of men, and they shall kill him; and after that he is killed, he shall rise the third day. But they understood not that saying, and were afraid to ask him. And he came to Capernaum: and being in the house he asked them, What was it that ye disputed among yourselves by the way? But they held their peace: for by the way they had disputed among themselves, who should be the greatest. And he sat down, and called the twelve, and saith unto them, If any man desire to be first, the same shall be last of all, and servant of all. And he took a child, and set him in the midst of them: and when he had taken him in his arms, he said unto them, Whosoever shall receive one of such children in my*

name, receiveth me: and whosoever shall receive me, receiveth not me, but him that sent me. *And John answered him, saying, Master, we saw one casting out devils in thy name, and he followeth not us: and we forbad him, because he followeth not us.* But Jesus said, Forbid him not: for there is no man which shall do a miracle in my name, that can lightly speak evil of me. For he that is not against us is on our part.

Mark 14:6-9 *And Jesus said, Let her alone; why trouble ye her? She hath wrought a good work on me.* For ye have the poor with you always, and whensoever ye will ye may do them good: but me ye have not always. She hath done what she could: she is come aforehand to anoint my body to the burying. Verily I say unto you, Wheresoever this gospel shall be preached throughout the whole world, this also that she hath done shall be spoken of for a memorial of her.

Women beyond the veil

The veil has been split, and now there is freedom to communicate with God, through Christ. The veil separated the pew from the power, through the priest when Christ embraced love and took up the cross. The curtain became nullified, the earth split, but the symbol of the cross bridged the gap. We are free in Christ, and there are no exclusive rights of man – we are all living by grace and walking by faith. Women have the ability to directly connect with God, through Christ – beyond the veil.

> *Matthew 27:51 And, behold, the **veil** of the temple was rent in twain from the top to the bottom; and the earth did quake, and the rocks rent;*

> *Mark 15:38 And the **veil** of the temple was rent in twain from the top to the bottom.*

*Luke 23:45 And the sun was darkened, and the **veil** of the temple was rent in the midst.*

*2 Corinthians 3:12-18 Seeing then that we have such hope, we use great plainness of speech: And not as Moses, which put a vail over his face, that the children of Israel could not stedfastly look to the end of that which is abolished: But their minds were blinded: for until this day remaineth the same vail untaken away in the reading of the old testament; which vail is done away in Christ. But even unto this day, when Moses is read, the vail is upon their heart. **Nevertheless when it shall turn to the Lord, the vail shall be taken away.** Now the Lord is that Spirit: and where the Spirit of the Lord is, there is liberty. But we all, with open face beholding as in a glass the glory of the Lord, are changed into the same image from glory to glory, even as by the Spirit of the Lord.*

31

May God continue to open our minds to the light of divine love, peace, and joy.

Isaiah **55:6-13** *Seek ye the LORD while he may be found, call ye upon him while he is near: Let the wicked forsake his way, and the unrighteous man his thoughts: and let him return unto the LORD, and he will have mercy upon him; and to our God, for he will abundantly pardon. For my thoughts are not your thoughts, neither are your ways my ways, saith the LORD. For as the heavens are higher than the earth, so are my ways higher than your ways, and my thoughts than your thoughts. For as the rain cometh down, and the snow from heaven, and returneth not thither, but watereth the earth, and maketh it bring forth and bud, that it may give seed to the sower, and bread to the eater: So shall my word be that goeth forth out of my mouth: it shall not return unto me void, but it shall accomplish that which I please, and it shall prosper in the thing whereto I sent it. For ye shall go out with joy, and be led forth with peace: the* *mountains and the hills shall break forth before you into singing, and all the trees of the field shall clap their hands. Instead of the thorn shall come up the fir tree, and instead of the brier shall come up the myrtle tree: and it shall be to the LORD for a name, for an everlasting sign that shall not be cut off.*

Preach or Teach, Teach?
The Great Commission

Matthew 28:18-20 And Jesus came and spake unto them, saying, All power is given unto me in heaven and in earth. Go ye therefore, and teach all nations, baptizing them in the name of the Father, and of the Son, and of the Holy Ghost: Teaching them to observe all things whatsoever I have commanded you: and, lo, I am with you alway, even unto the end of the world. Amen.

It seems that the main church event is the Sunday sermon, some pastors are hired and fired based on the ability to present a good sermon. People come to hear the choir and the sermon – there is a great amount of pressure placed on the pastor to preach. Although we seem to favor preaching, Christ commissioned us to teach.

The sermon seems even more central within charismatic and non-European traditions, whereby ministers are expected to bring forth a rhythmic melodious conclusion that sparks a shouting congregation. Although much time and effort is placed within the Sunday worship experience so the crowd will return – Bible study and Sunday school along with other Bible learning opportunities are often poorly attended. We know that there are times when preaching is defined as teaching, but it seems that many preachers are mostly interested in the WOW and not the WORD of GOD. The wow seeks to entertain and keep people coming back through entertaining emotional empowerment, whereby the moment is great, but the life-changing impact is unsustained. Teaching versus preaching seems to imply that someone is learning, whereby preaching may not always bring forth the same connotation. It is more than difficult to reach a destination if we don't first determine where we want to go – therefore it seems plausible to say that a sermon must be developed with teaching and learning in mind. Teaching must be an important component of the church – as Christ repeatedly makes the command to teach. Many of the issues within the church come forth from a lack of knowledge (Hosea 4:6). We must teach the way of Christ carefully placing the scriptures above our traditions and American culture. We must seek to start with scripture, as we follow through under the direction of the Holy Spirit.

I would contend that we must prepare the church through teaching. To set forth the foundation for any great movement within the church in order to execute God's word, we must first know it. Stories have been told and books have been published presenting the widespread conflict within churches across the country. Unbelievably, churches are suing pastors and vice versa – which reflects our failure to teach 1Corinthians chapter six. We must have the capacity to teach beyond physical, spiritual, social, economic, and cultural conflicts, we must teach with an expectation that the scriptures will bring forth the wisdom necessary for a viable movement of the church.

New members must be received into a teaching environment, which promotes participation from the commencement of connection. We must present an expectation for new members to become incorporated into the congregation through learning. Many new members that happily come through the front door, later tip silently out of the back, never to return. Most of the time people leave because of their unfulfilled expectations. People often join a congregation with the perception that the church is a perfect place filled with perfect people; unfortunately they become withdrawn as soon as they discover imperfections. The church must be honest in order to impart a realistic perception of the congregation and Christian life. Our church teaches/disciples new members during a four-week class designed to introduce our congregation along with our core beliefs and values. We seek to convey our truest self, new members are introduced to our strong attributes and we outline the things that we are working to improve. It's best to tell people the truth. If the church is cliquish and unfriendly new members need to be made aware, so that they may know what to expect as our congregations work through issues. Churches are not perfect, yet there are always parts of us that are more than wonderful. People join because they are attracted to something about a congregation, therefore we should not embrace trepidation with regards to revealing our true self.

Christ tells us twice to teach in Matthew 28:18-20, we must recognize that it becomes our responsibility to teach the church to fine tune our lives, as we are admonished to teach the observance of all things. We can teach our way past church financial strain and poor giving units, as we teach members the importance of caring for the ministry.

We can teach past poor attendance and participation – whatever issue, the church may always teach the truth of the scripture in order to overcome obstacles. We often rely on prayer alone without work, when we should continue to have faith through prayer and obey the words of Christ: teaching converts to invest in the way of the scriptures.

Many churches struggle to remain unified; often ministry boards and pastors are at odds. I have had a number of experiences with church unrest, both through connections with other congregations, and through my service as a pastor – as we often try to pray, fight, sing, preach, love, and whatever else through issues it seems that we need to always incorporate teaching. I can physically strike the gavel in a heated church business meeting, but it's best when the congregation is struck through the scriptures, as God's word will always precisely rectify our situations (Hebrews 4:12).

Christ was not always liked

Luke 23:21 But they cried, saying, Crucify him, crucify him.

When Christ confronted the money changers and healed the afflicted in Matthew 21:12, religious leaders were displeased. When Christ taught in the synagogue in Luke 4:29, the congregants sought to throw him off of a cliff. Far too often the church works too hard to be liked by all – when Christ was often disliked. Paul and many of the early church leaders were disliked, yet the modern church seems to be moved to appease socio-cultural powers through pluralistic politically correct rhetoric. The Gospel seems to be under censorship, as the church seeks to be viable through motivational messages that exclude subjects that may cause spiritual discomfort. I've even heard pastors explain multi-faith church models, whereby people of mixed faiths make up the congregation – the scriptures seem to strongly convey that Christ is the only way; Christianity is founded upon a monotheistic foundation; it takes a lot of interpretation to arrive at a multi-faith construction. It seems that the church must embrace the scriptures, even when the connection is not popular. Although this may lead to unpopularity it will lead us away from the politically correct slaves that many of us have become.

Unfortunately, success in ministry is far too often measured by the number of congregants, income, building size, and the pastor's popularity – when the church should be considered successful when it is aligned with the scriptures like Christ, through the guidance of the Holy Spirit. At times the Gospel will not be popular, but it will always be powerful. We must seek to walk in freedom, and truth is the chief agent of liberation. The truth is the best image to present, in order for each of us to compare ourselves to God's standard – the Bible admonishes us to examine ourselves as we enter into communion with Christ and each other (1 Corinthians 11:28). We must allow the truth of the scriptures to present us with God's image for us. In order to emulate Christ, we must first see Him.

It is almost unbelievable, that congregants wanted to throw Christ off of a cliff – it would seem that they would have welcomed the presence of the messiah, reading from the scriptures and proclaiming the truth. There are modern churches where Christ and the truth are not welcome – notice he was teaching, and not entertaining. Singing is good, and lifting our voices through the melodic art of song is a viable part of worship; however our churches must be more than concert centers. There are times when worship seems like a production and although we should be prepared and rehearsed – worship has to be more than a theatrically melodic production.

Bless us, but hold the change

Change is an important part of God's process for our lives. In order for us to be truly blessed by the Lord we must be willing to allow the Holy Spirit to guide us through the process of transformation – which is inextricably connected with our blessings. I am not saying that we should change for change's sake; or we should create an atmosphere of self imposed change, I'm saying that we are on a journey from the bondage of evil toward the freedom of God's family. Each day we should strive to become more and more like Christ, through the power of the Holy Spirit. The more our lives are constructed toward God's plan, the more we will experience the blessings of God.

Growth is too costly – Abraham and Lot

Genesis 13:6-8 And the land was not able to bear them, that they might dwell together: for their substance was great, so that they could not dwell together. And there was a strife between the herdmen of Abram's cattle and the herdmen of Lot's cattle: and the Canaanite and the Perizzite dwelled then in the land. And Abram said unto Lot, Let there be no strife, I pray thee, between me and thee, and between my herdmen and thy herdmen; for we be brethren.

Far too often we want the blessings, but we don't want the change. There are some churches that are afraid of growth because it requires change. Conflict arises because there will be too many of us to get along: if the church grows there will not be enough spotlight left for me. In the situation between Lot and Abraham it seems that they did not exchange any words of conflict, the unrest emerged from outside forces (Genesis 13). The church must beware of outsiders' devilish intentions. Although it seems unconscionable, there are other church members and pastors who see a growing healthy church as competition. Because it is the church we often look naively upon congregations as a group of people in love with the will and way of God, yet there were people in Biblical antiquity that sought to throw Christ off a cliff after his sermonic pontification. We can never think that the devilish forces will leave the church alone – in fact it seems plausible to deduce that the forces of evil will wage war upon the righteous even more when the favor and blessings of God are upon the church. Sometime other congregations will produce negative propaganda against another church that seems a threat to competitive conniving cancerous conductors.

We must teach the necessity to guard our hearts and minds against the outsiders who seek to create conflict within the church. It is important to point out that not all words are true, even when it comes from those who have attended church for a great number of years. We must examine all by the word of God (1 John 4:1), when people using cunning deceptive words that seek to divide congregations, and keep negative gossip circulating – we should automatically recognize the imprint of evil. Even when legitimate concerns arise congregations must keep family business within the family, refusing to let others dig for and/or manipulate information. In many families there are two primary rules – family business stays in the family and we may talk about family, but nobody else can! We should not promote negative talk about our church or pastor – especially with outsiders (even when they may seem knowledgeable about a particular subject). God will bless us with positive change, yet we must be ready to receive the great responsibility that comes with blessings.

The big and the small

I have heard pastors and members bashing each other over the size of congregations. It seems to me that size is not a major factor, churches big and small go bankrupt and/or close based on demographics, mismanagement, and a variety of other factors. I have witnessed churches go through a merger and eventually end up being absorbed by another congregation – churches change, just as the Israelites, Disciples of John and Christ, and the early church did. The church is an organism, as we are the body of Christ – and seasons come and go. Based on my armchair analysis, I would think that more churches with less than 100 members close than larger congregations. We must be careful to evaluate issues within a *gestaltian* methodological framework, as we approach popularized fragments of church news panhandled by atheistic reporters. There is a price for ministry great or small, as the text encourages us to count the cost[4] - which may be interpreted in a multitude of applications, yet it seems to me that the root of the admonishment emerges from the soil of stewardship. Although stewardship is a factor there are so many other factors that contribute to sustained vitality within a church – there are very few churches older than 100; and even fewer older than 200. Just as people have an appointed time to die, there comes a time when the organism of the church comes to an end of a lifecycle. People connect with God in different ways – big, grand, opulent, and other like words are relative to the beholding interpreter. Some people connect with God in large fellowships, and others prefer smaller fellowship – interestingly, budgets are not necessarily determined by the number of persons within the congregation; it is more accurately evaluated by the economy of the membership. The magnitude of the tallest Baptist church in New York, did not derive from many patron saints – but just one man named John Rockefeller.

---

[4] Luke 14:28

Additionally, just as I am practically sure there were some who questioned Christ feeding the multitude – did they really need to eat? Couldn't he have just preached and sent them home? Did he have to turn water into wine – the wedding could have gone on dry? Something that seems unnecessary to some, may be essential to the faith of others. I remain prayerful for churches that are going through the strain of recession (big and small), as I recognize that we are all in this together. There are crooks in ministries of all sizes, and God will deal with them in due time – we can find thieves, pedophiles, rapists, liars, and a number of other transgressors leading churches through a destructive path. Yet, we must remain prayerful and jubilant toward the work of God – even when we don't understand it. Limiting God in the life of others may cause the Lord to limit redemptive power in our personal lives. Let us strive to build the kingdom of God through powerful encouragement and not negative notions that destroy the movement of the church.

Losing Ishmael

The hard part of any story is trying to figure out where to began, and this story is no different – so I'll try to start with the beginning.

The media, or as my community calls it, the news, makes the world seem like a dangerous, cold, callous, and hurtful social mechanism that produces diseased people. At times our society seems extremely depressed, as we seek after "the dream" – striving to win the rat race. Although all of us are on some type of quest or journey, it seems that some of us have not questioned our purpose for traveling, but instead seriously projected our final destination without deliberate thought. Years ago there was a movie entitled *Mahogany* staring Diana Ross and Billy Dee Williams – the characters both had dreams that they were attempting to accomplish, yet it took time for them to recognize that a dream is only a nightmare when the purpose of the journey is missing. The theme song of the movie *Mahogany* was appropriately titled "Do You Know Where You're Going To?"

The things you don't want or don't care about seem to come easy and your desires seem to be so hard to reach. Additionally, it becomes even harder to understand why those who do not value their resources most often seem to have exactly what we want. Life becomes even more difficult when we get to borrow what we want in life only to lose it. One Monday in the 1980s people were figuratively jumping out of windows and plunging to the death as the stock market fell drastically. Those suicidal people were suffering from the loss of borrowed money. Sadly they had held an illusion of ownership – when all along they did not have the ultimate power over anything except internal feelings that they surrendered to destructive forces.

Many motivational speakers promulgate a "dream achieving gospel," however it seems that the first important step is to determine the plausibility of a dream's capacity to become reality. Furthermore, what will fundamentally change if the dream becomes reality, and does the final production fulfill a greater purpose? Normally we think that our final destination is happiness, joy, and peace – the only problem seems to be the fact that these are internal feelings that we often believe are controlled by external forms –"things," "stuff," "trinkets," "tokens" (you get the point).

If we really want happiness, then how can we get it? The fact is we cannot control our feelings based on the things we own, and/or the relationships we have. We cannot work everything out on our own; the good times are determined by our relationship with God. No matter how hard we try, we don't have the power to independently sustain any part of our life. When we do things "our way," ultimately everything ends "our way" – destructive, demented, and depressed! I have found doing things my way is a waste of time and energy. Hence, our story begins with a man like me – attempting to execute God's promise, using alternative plans. When God makes us a promise we must allow God to plan the journey.

Abram/Abraham is a primary character within the text of three major religions, (Judaism, Christianity, and Islam) and his journey with God is a foundation to all relationships with God after his (Abram's) time period. Abram lived in a town called Ur, and one day he had an encounter with a supernatural force that persuaded him to ascribe to one God (monotheism) as opposed to the popular belief in many gods (polytheism). The practice of believing in more than one god is theoretically foreign in our modern society – however it seems that materialism is closely related if not the same thing. We worship houses, cars, money, people, clothes, and etceteras. Things that cannot consistently keep us happy, joyful, and/or at peace. Although Abram lived in the midst of people that placed their hope across a vast array of gods – he chose to follow the voice of one God.

The way things were

Abram was seventy-five years old, married, without children – his father and brother had died - and then he heard the voice of God. Often it is after the death of familiar voices that we hear the voice of God. Can you imagine what it would be like to live in a society that treasures childbirth as we do money and prestige – and not be able to have any treasures, after seventy-five years of life?

Not long ago I heard a young woman say that she didn't want to live beyond 30 years old without being married. I could relate, because marriage has always seemed like the ultimate lifestyle to me, and in fact it is –

as the Bible seems to suggest that a man needs a woman and vice versa. Man was noticeably alone, and God created out of man a woman. Although the institution of marriage is holy and right before God, it can also be disastrous if God is not the creator within the relationship. We can become as Abram, living in a town full of gods (false powers and securities), and yet unable to create a sustainable future.

The death of Abram's father cut him off from the wisdom of the past and the absence of children cut him off from the joy of the future. Life is often wedged between a rock and a hard place when your past fades and your future dissipates into the pale abyss of a perpetual midnight with bleak hopes miscarried over the realism of a seventy-five-year-old barren existence. What happens when your nothing is greater than your lack, when life is at the bottom and the foundation of your pit gives way to an even deeper reality? I understand what it means to long for a family, and many of my days have been spent asking God for the joy of family.

After a certain age we start to seek the innate purpose to produce that which is within us, as we are all pregnant with purpose and potential. Some of us may seek after education, others financial wealth, some philanthropy, and a few just seek what we call a modest living – but the need for connection normally overarches our journey.

We share the need to produce, just as Abram; however, there are times when life seems to hold us hostage. Our problems have a way of seeming much greater than our possibilities. Could you imagine what it would feel like to reach the age of seventy-five years old and the most important parts of life have not manifested? Each of us reaches a point in life where it seems that we are at the end of our rope and life has left us short changed at the checkout counter.

The call

Abram heard the voice of God, and was moved to embark on a great life-altering journey. It seems to me that his faith was great; however he often had moments of misdirection. Abram had to be ready to move forward on the voice – far too often we are only moved by the visible and not the voiced. We live in an age whereby we embrace the philosophy that seeing is believing – when the more important things in life are felt and not seen. All that we see and know started with the voice of God, as we may witness within the first chapter of the Bible. We may also recognize that the Gospel of John chapter 1 reflects that in the beginning was the word, and the word was with God, and the word was God – but how many of us value God's word enough to be moved by words, without seeing visible signs of confirmation. Many times in our life we must be willing to move on God's voice alone – as we will often be blind to the full future manifestation. When children are given a directive, if they don't act on the voice of their parent then oftentimes punishment will become manifested. Many times we ignore the voice in order to seek a sign – only to witness manifested punishment as an alternative to the blessing that would have accompanied obedience to God's voice. We must be willing to surrender and pack for the purposeful journey that God will lead us through even when we cannot see where we are being led.

Abram was on his way to what most if not all of us want – he was on his way to fulfillment; although he did not know the means of his journey or how long it would take. The Lord has a plan and purpose for us both individually and collectively – however we are often so busy planning the trip that we miss the divine journey. Moreover, our senses are so overwhelmed with a variety of technological devices which seem to paralyze our ability to retain awareness toward the movement of God through the power of scriptures magnified by the Holy Spirit.

Our attention spans have deteriorated with the modern era of technology. Less than a few decades ago, people were fascinated by the radio and were moved toward great moments of imagination. Even after the development of television, people were not continually cerebrally connected; as programming was extremely limited even when I was a child, broadcasting was interrupted from midnight until dawn. There was time to hear the voice of God, there was time to appreciate the beauty of creation. Think how hard it would have been for Abram to hear the Lord over the call of a second job, the music blasting from his headphones, the vibration of his cellular phone – capturing signals between calls and text. We must learn to make our global communicative part-time and embrace full-time communication with God through the Holy Spirit. Let us remember that Abram's journey commenced with the voice of God, as did all of creation – we must hear from the Lord.

Allow travel time

I used to greatly dislike the admonishment to allow travel time, as these words were often nagging reminders presented by my maternal grandmother. Whenever we would get ready to go somewhere she would rush us with the notice that we had to allow for travel time. It seems that when God speaks to us, we often neglect to allow for travel time. In the book of Genesis chapter 12, Abram hears from God – moves from his hometown, hears from God again – builds an altar and calls on the name of the Lord; but leaves the altar before hearing from God again. Abram ended up in negative situations every time he neglected to obtain full instructions from God. Oftentimes we hear from God and run to action before the Lord gives us completed instructions.

The Lord often gives us several opportunities to learn from our mistakes, as consequences should help to teach us the error of our ways. Abram should have learned from his mistakes, yet it seems that he continued to use part of God's promise – and move prematurely. Uncorrected small issues generally escalate into bigger issues with grander consequences. God even changed Abram's name to Abraham, which should have provided him with renewed hope toward the blessings that were to come. Although Abraham had faith great enough to follow God away from his hometown – his faith seemed to waver under the pressure of time, and his wife's voice. Abraham became involved with a woman (Egyptian) outside of his marriage in order to have a child, as he and his wife seemed to have gotten tired of waiting on God to send a child through their marriage. I would think that Abraham should have noticed that every time he fooled with all things Egyptian, he ended up in a situation – but similar to us he keeps making the same mistake. Allow travel time, when God takes us on a journey; don't become so fixated upon the prophetic fulfillment that you become tempted to take shortcuts.

Looks okay

Ishmael was born illegitimately to Abraham, and the text suggests that things went well for a while – there were excited feelings of accomplishment with the newness of life. Unfortunately, the family was soon thrust into a season of dysfunction as Abraham's wife and baby's mama became irritated by each other. Eventually, Abraham had to send the other woman and his son away, in order to save his marriage and restore the relationship with his wife. God's original plan ultimately became manifested, as Abraham and his wife produced a son named Isaac.

Abraham lost Ishmael, as we often lose the products of our plans. We produce Ishmaels when we fail to wait on God's way, and conjure ways to reach false fulfillment using our engineered methods. Some of us are in forged relationships, living in temporary mansions, driving the wrong car – because we fail to fully wait upon the completed way of God in our lives. We love our children, but there are a number of people caring for kids that they did not intend to have – and if the truth be told there are a great number of Ishmaels.

Some churches seem to be producing Ishmaels – buildings, money, political power, prestigious/well-known ministers, television shows, and people pumped up on entertaining self-serving religion. The church should always be connected to God and the way of Christ, through the direction of the Holy Spirit. The church cannot truly produce without the power of God. When we create schemes to go around the Lord and partnerships that produce faux church experiences we will ultimately lose Ishmael. Although there are many times when we grow weary of waiting on God we should continue to wait, as the consequences of premature actions and/or disobedience are not worth the trouble.

Other Thoughts

Don't forget to move – Israel famine and Egypt

Genesis 42:5 And the sons of Israel came to buy corn among those that came: for the famine was in the land of Canaan.

The Egyptians were living in an established location with established cities; on the other hand Jacob's family did not seem to be permanently connected to a specific land (Genesis 41, 42). It seems plausible that people permanently connected to an established location would be subject to a food shortage – but, I've often wondered how a nomadic cultural paradigm could lead to a state of famine. It seems like Jacob's family may not have been afflicted by the famine if they would have kept moving. Furthermore, it seems that they stayed too long in Egypt; although the Egyptians welcomed Jacob's family in the beginning because of Joseph – as time went on Jacob's descendants were enslaved. The church could learn a lot from observing the cycles of Jacob's family, as congregations create traditions that often seem to repress positive movement. The church must pay attention to the seasons that God orchestrates. Just because our metaphoric Egypt may be the vehicle of favor for a season, things change. Echoing through churches across the country we can hear the words: "We've always done it that way!" or "We've never done it that way!" – sometimes we hold to a non-Biblical tradition.

Spiritual movement is generally our only focus, when there are times when we need a physical move; unfortunately the average church is not prepared to physically move. Established churches are often afflicted with conflict when even prompted to think about physically moving. A building can be as old as the pyramids, with a leaking roof, faulty plumbing, and a third of the facility has been condemned with yellow warning tape – and attached members will see it as a capital offence to think about the acquisition of a more suitable property. The front entrance of an old church has been condemned for years and the congregation has been unable to afford the reconstruction. The same church has declining attendance in a building where water stains are visible fixtures on the ceiling. The community has rejected the church by petitioning to limit their on-street parking – as I am not the pastor of that church, I cannot categorically say that it is time to think about some changes; it seems evidentiary.

During a real estate market decline, a growing church was given a divine opportunity to purchase property three times larger than a building they had outgrown. Through a corporate donation, nearly a half million dollars was reduced from the price, and the church could purchase a new building for less than the value of their original building. One would think that the entire congregation would have been excited over such a great blessing, yet nearly a fourth of the membership launched a revolt against the pastor and supporting members. Even when it seems that the hand of God is easy to see, there are elements of evil that may emerge.

There are times when a community has moved beyond our expertise as fishers of men – the fish that we are gifted to catch have moved upstream; while our nets are empty downstream. Churches must remain in tune with the Holy Spirit in order to know when to stay and when to move. Staying too long in one place may lead to famine and slavery. Even though a particular location had been good for us in the past we must remain willing to move forward.

There's a time for plows and a time for swords

Joel 3:10 Beat your plowshares into swords, and your pruning hooks into spears: let the weak say, I am strong.

The traditions of the church can keep us plowing when we need to reevaluate our position and update our resources. The Israelites were instructed to take their agricultural resources and reshape them into weapons for battle. The church must practice good resource management. We must allow the Holy Spirit to lead us though seasons of change. Our socio-economic environment is rapidly transforming, churches frequently stay the same traditional antiquated constructions. The church often uses the reality of a changeless God to validate a changeless church – when in fact we need to theologically realize that our premise is always wrong when we think that we are the same as God; when in fact

God is powerfully perfect and we are not. We often become captured by delusions of grandeur, believing that we are ontologically superior to God – when in fact we were not eyewitnesses to creation. Therefore we should never become exclusive thinkers, moving outside of God's direction for the church. In order for the church to become Christlike, change is more than necessary. There is a time for harvesting, and there are seasons of preparation whereby we must restructure our resources, just as was mandated in Joel 3:10.

It is more than difficult to face the need for change, it often seems easy to stay the same – as very little work is needed to sustain status quo. When change takes place in a church, it becomes difficult because oftentimes it means people have to be re-arranged and/or re-taught. Many church folks don't like giving up their plowshares and pruning hooks – as it requires relinquishing authority toward a new way. Churches would find change easier if continual focus remained upon God, and individuals were taught that leadership within a single ministry paradigm is not your last destination. The church must have a process that is accommodating toward change – therefore we should never focus on the manifested resources of God more than we focus on God, and the wisdom that we are given through the Holy Spirit to use divine gifts. The church must continually be reminded that the blessing is not in the plowshares or the swords – the blessing is in the provider of the metal! We should not care about the shape of our resources, as long as we know that God has engineered the process.

Many churches have all of the resources for worship: ministers, choirs, ushers, instruments, Bibles, hymn books, etc. Nevertheless, the church is in decline with great resources, because we lack the wisdom to use the gifts that God has given us. In John 21:6 the disciples illustrate how simple the process may be; cast your nets on the other side. The disciples had all the necessary resources to catch fish, and the fish were there – all they needed was the Messiah's instructions. The modern church continues to need divine instructions. We are merely wasting our time when we attempt to be productive using our own instructions. Although a man's ways seem right from his own point of view, it is God's point of view that we need (Proverbs 21:2). I am sure that many congregations do not even recognize the degenerative movements within the church – because from the inside we keep looking inside, when we need the Holy Spirit to show us what we look like from the outside looking in.

There are times when God wants us to lead, and times when we must follow – Joel 3:10, says let the weak say I am strong. Far too often the leadership within the church becomes stagnated because some antique, overeducated know it all, loud aggressive, and/or big money person will not relinquish authority. We have to train the weak to become the strong, the church should be a place of empowering encouragement that fosters the work of the Holy Spirit in each of us to develop the gifts that God has placed within us. There is a season for the unique plethora of gifts that co-exist within the church. We must seek the guidance of the Holy Spirit to appropriately release each of our gifts according to God's time and purpose within the congregation and community.

Keep building, just stay on the rock

Matthew 16:18 And I say also unto thee, That thou art Peter, and upon this rock I will build my church; and the gates of hell shall not prevail against it.

Christ is building the church, we must realize that we are a work in progress and our primary task is to stay upon the rock; we must continually remain in relationship with Christ. Not all change is good change, not every voice we hear is the voice of God. In order for us to embrace necessary change, we must fervently study the scriptures. The Bible provides the blueprint for the Holy Spirit to interpret for us. The Bible joined with the guidance of the Holy Spirit helps us to stay on the rock – knowing the voice, will, and way of God.

When Christ is the chief architect, the evil forces may come against the church, but the evil forces will not prevail against the people of God – constructed upon the rock. There is great consolation in the fact that the church upon the rock is touchable, but not destructible – we may stand upon the scripture come hell or high water! Tough times will come in the life of the church, conflict will arise – stay on the rock! We will be criticized if we do not conform to the ways of the world and the pressures of societal norms – but stay on the rock! The pew and the preacher will disagree at times – but stay on the rock! People will favor sermons that validate sin, and gild the Gospel – but, hallelujah; stay on the rock!

Do we need that?

Many congregations struggle with how to align resources with ministry. Some members will want to make a specific purchase and others will say it is unnecessary. Pastors and ministry leaders are often challenged to make bricks without straw like Hebrew slaves – even when our budgets have been cut to reflect our facts and not our faith. God has a plan that uniquely shapes each church for ministry – cost should never be the primary question; we should always ask is this what God wants? If the Lord has ordained and commissioned the work, then cost is not a factor. The church must always work from the economy of The Kingdom and not the banks of the world. Whatever God says, our faith must line up – even when our facts seem contrary.

Water is good for you, let them drink that!

John 2:7-11 Jesus saith unto them, Fill the waterpots with water. And they filled them up to the brim. 8 And he saith unto them, Draw out now, and bear unto the governor of the feast. And they bare it. 9 When the ruler of the feast had tasted the water that was made wine, and knew not whence it was: (but the servants which drew the water knew;) the governor of the feast called the bridegroom, 10 And saith unto him, Every man at the beginning doth set forth good wine; and when men have well drunk, then that which is worse: but thou hast kept the good wine until now. 11 This beginning of miracles did Jesus in Cana of Galilee, and manifested forth his glory; and his disciples believed on him.

Countless denominations of Christians can re-tell the first miracle of the Messiah, but consider the narrative rated X for its alcohol content. I have even heard some say that it wasn't really wine – it was what we call grape juice, proclaiming that the terms were interchangeable back then. Many congregants try to distance themselves from things they don't understand, don't like, or don't agree with – and unfortunately there are times when interpretation articulates the text out of contextual character. John 2:7-11 seems to emerge in simplicity and we may walk away with five summary words; Jesus turned water into wine. Many church folks are always poised to ask do we need that; it seems too secular or non-essential?

Christ's first recorded miracle demonstrates His use of the seemingly nonessential to bring forth glory and belief. Not only did Christ use what some modern members would have called a waste of the miraculous – He didn't reveal the great deed to the powerful guests of the feast, but to the servants and His disciples. Christ reveals that the church must be of service, and at times the insignificant may be used to show servants the magnificent. The Lord will make a way out of no way – fill the pots with water and have faith. There are times when church budgets must be filled with water, waiting on the hand of the Lord to bring forth manifested substance. When we wait on the movement of Christ through the Holy Spirit, not only will He bless us – it will be far better than what we could self-produce. The latter wine was better than the first – have faith for ministry, the best is yet to come!

The church must not try to make itself look good, the church does not have to ring its own bell – the church can only truly shine when the Lord turns on the heavenly light. In so many words the governor told the bridegroom that he saved the best for last and commended him for being different from others. The bridegroom was noted as an out of the box man, bringing forth progressively better hospitality as the festivities endured.

Congregations should learn to stand forth as this bridegroom, allowing Christ to bless and promote the church. The church that embraces Christ as a part of the guest list will never run out of vigor and vitality – the feast will proceed. The governor conveyed that the latter was better than the first. The church should always be better, because we should be transformed to invite Christ to take control more and more as we embrace the guidance of the Holy Spirit.

Church or restaurant

John 6:2-13 And a great multitude followed him, because they saw his miracles which he did on them that were diseased. 3 And Jesus went up into a mountain, and there he sat with his disciples. 4 And the Passover, a feast of the Jews, was nigh. 5 When Jesus then lifted up his eyes, and saw a great company come unto him, he saith unto Philip, Whence shall we buy bread, that these may eat? 6 And this he said to prove him: for he himself knew what he would do. 7 Philip answered him, Two hundred pennyworth of bread is not sufficient for them, that every one of them may take a little. 8 One of his disciples, Andrew, Simon Peter's brother, saith unto him, 9 There is a lad here, which hath five barley loaves, and two small fishes: but what are they among so many? 10 And Jesus said, Make the men sit down. Now there was much grass in the place. So the men sat down, in number about five thousand. 11 And Jesus took the loaves; and when he had given thanks, he distributed to the disciples, and the disciples to them that were set down; and likewise of the fishes as much as they would. 12 When they were filled, he said unto his disciples, Gather up the fragments that remain, that nothing be lost. 13 Therefore they gathered them together, and filled twelve baskets with the fragments of the five barley loaves, which remained over and above unto them that had eaten.

The disciples show us that we are not the first to have budget issues, we are not the first to have doubts, and we are not the first to struggle with ministry. Christ was the greatest preacher and teacher, yet He wanted to physically feed the multitude. With the mentality of many parishioners, I am sure that if Christ were leading a modern church someone would have told Him to just preach. Congregations often want ministers to just preach and leave everything else to us. Why do we need bread?

Why do we need fish? Just preach! Why do we need to paint the sanctuary, just preach! Why do we need new hymn books, just preach! Why do we need a projector, PowerPoint, computers, and technicians; just preach! Why should we be concerned about the community, the hungry, the poor, or the marginalized; just preach! Why do we need bread and fish?

Christ was positioned to feed the multitude with or without the disciples, as a matter of fact He already knew that His plan would have to save the day beyond the disciples' inadequacy. Where our money runs out, Christ has a plan; all we have to do is allow the Holy Spirit to instruct us within the plan. The people were hungry and the scriptures seem to suggest that the disciples were not actively positive toward feeding them. The people are hungry today and it seems that many of our churches are not actively positive toward the command of Christ to love our neighbors as we love ourselves. Christ says make them sit down – our churches have left multitudes standing in need. We must make them sit down and show them the love of Christ before we embrace the ideology that we must fill them full of as many regurgitated scriptures that we can remember from Sunday school. We must love them and not leave them; we must serve them and not sever them. We must open our pews to the least, lost, defensive, destructive, dysfunctional, marginal, migrated, hungry, hurt, enslaved, and the empty – let them sit with us; compel them to sit with us.

We don't need bread, which is non-essential to ministry – just preach! Christ asked the disciple where to buy bread – the disciple's incongruent answer was aligned with money; not ministry. The Messiah was asking where, not how much – far too often the Lord is asking us one thing while we are too focused on something else. We must be willing to sit them down, even when we may not know the next step, as long as the first step is divinely directed – then the next step is sure to follow. God has not brought us this far to leave us; we must continue to follow the lead of the scriptures through the guidance of the Holy Spirit. God will take care of you, all the way!

Church is a place where old people go to be right, and young people go to keep silent. Young people help us to keep good Sunday School attendance numbers, and make us feel accomplished during Vacation Bible School. It seems that young people are often thought of as the church of tomorrow, and disregarded as marginally unimportant. The miraculous ministry of God can use anybody, and can never be limited. Joel 2:28 tells us that God will pour out the Spirit upon all flesh – transuding gender, age, and/or socio-economic status. We must recognize the lad within John 6:9 has the material Christ chooses to use. The grown leaders said they didn't have sufficient resources, but there is a lad. How many of our churches have disregarded the lad and his lunch? The younger generation has gifted contributions for the church and we must be willing to allow the Holy Spirit to direct us toward a church that can inclusively embrace the rich diversity of thought that our young people bring to the congregation.

There will be times when the resources we have to work with will seem inadequate – the lad's lunch must have seemed as crumbs when paralleled with the multitude. Christ models the first step toward increased capacity, start with thankfulness. The church must be willing to do the work of Christ, and thankful for all that we have been given. We should stop complaining, and appreciate the resources that the Lord has provided – and the greatest resource is the Lord's presence. So what if the church down the street has pews and you have folding chairs, so what if they have more parking and you have to park on the grass, so what if someone else has a grand pulpit and you have a music stand – be thankful for the opportunity to serve and be thankful for all that God has provided even when the resources seem small. Miracles happen when we stop leaning on our ways, and fully trust his way – sit them down and wait for the next instruction.

Symbolically this passage brings forth great joy and hope, as it seems to me that the bread itself speaks volumes. The loaves were created from barley, which was the first harvest of the year, around the season of Passover as the scriptures articulate. These loaves symbolically represent the first of the season and not the last, oh if I were preaching right now – this would be what we call a shouting point! Let me say it again; these loaves symbolically represent the first of the season and not the last (meaning, this is just the appetizer – there is more to come). The loaves were not the main event, the barley harvest was first – other seasons will bring more delectable harvest. Sit them down and give them an appetizer, give them a bit of bread and some fish – that will get their attention, but the word of Christ will capture their heart. The bread was a signal that more was to come; the fish was a symbol of the Christ who died for me – our great Messiah. Ixthus (Greek word for fish) was a symbol of the Messiah, as an acrostic message. The word "ixthus," emerges from five Greek letters, the first letter represented the word Jesus. The second letter represented the word Christ, the next two, God's Son, and the final letter represented the word Savior articulated as "Jesus Christ is God's Son, the Savior." Do we really need fish and bread? Hallelujah, the Savior leads us to sit them down and provide what may seem non-essential; so that divine work may be done. We may not understand it, but as long as God gets it we should always be alright with it.

There were twelve baskets let over, enough for each disciple to individually see the abundance that came forth through the power of Christ. The baskets represent the reciprocal virtue within Christ; He spoke and yet He listened – He gave and yet he received. God does not need our tithes and offerings – He appreciates our willingness to give back. The church should be a place of reciprocal relationships – we should speak, but we should also listen. We should heal, but we should also be healed. Give to the world, but collect the fragments – as they testify to the glory of God. Collecting the fragments seemed to spotlight the importance of good stewardship. The church should be giving, but not wasteful – congregations must reuse, recycle, and renew. There are times when congregations suffer lack because of wasteful behaviors – which normally stem from division. When ministries within the church collaborate and work together, resources are best managed. Little becomes much, when we place it within the master's hands.

Exclusive Inclusion or Extraordinary Exclusion

Sin in the church; my type or yours?

Matthew 23:23-28 Woe unto you, scribes and Pharisees, hypocrites! For ye pay tithe of mint and anise and cumin, and have omitted the weightier matters of the law, judgment, mercy, and faith: these ought ye to have done, and not to leave the other undone. Ye blind guides, which strain at a gnat, and swallow a camel. Woe unto you, scribes and Pharisees, hypocrites! For ye make clean the outside of the cup and of the platter, but within they are full of extortion and excess. Thou blind Pharisee, cleanse first that which is within the cup and platter, that the outside of them may be clean also. Woe unto you, scribes and Pharisees, hypocrites! For ye are like unto whited sepulchers, which indeed appear beautiful outward, but are within full of dead men's bones, and of all uncleanness. Even so ye also outwardly appear

righteous unto men, but within ye are full of
hypocrisy and iniquity.

We are living within a disturbing age, which seems to
present a number of pragmatic challenges toward
ministry. To sin or not to sin seems to be the question.
How should the church deal with the problem of sin,
especially in an age whereby it seems necessary to decide
which sins are acceptable and which ones must remain
hidden. In fact, it seems that there are some churches and
denominations being prompted to definitively define sin.
There are societal forces that have characteristically
demonized the church for making declarations against
issues that have been historically unacceptable as
normative interpretations of centralized Biblical
principles. I fully understand that there are times when
the Bible has been misinterpreted by a mass of scholars;
however it seems to me that we are on a slippery slope
when scriptural interpretation is altered based upon

91

mundane media sponsored by sinful sips of self sustaining syrup. The church used to hold a position of authority, whereby the greater society held components of doctrinal positions as sacred even when not popular – the church had an internal voice. It seems that modernity has presented the church with a script, and the doctrinal voice has become an external prompt that disregards the sanctity of the scriptures. It seems to me that the church has moved away from the responsibility to maintain the Bible as the *condicio sine qua non* (the central part that everything is dependent upon), as many churches have turned toward socio-economic approval to mark success in ministry.

We have new age Pharisees and Scribes that have learned to pimp the church as a streetwalker wearied by disease, yet tricked out with flashy garments that catch the eye. There is so much entertainment in many of our churches that the people in the pew have not come to realize the rip-off. I am not at all an advocate of bashing any particular church; therefore let me be clear – my statements are not aimed at a particular church, as I embrace the ideology that we are all in this together, and components of demonic damage seem to eat away at all of our churches. In the book of Matthew chapter 23, Jesus points out that we often focus on some things and leave other things undone. There is a great struggle in attempting to be a well rounded, healthy church that leaves nothing undone; however, Christ seems to advocate awareness over piety. Our problem is not squarely upon leaving some things undone – our problems emerge when we spotlight the things that we choose to do well, and minimize the things that we choose not to deal with.

I am willing to be transparent and risk a few friends by saying what some people would love to say, but they are too fearful to articulate – political correctness and satanic social justice in the modern context are barriers to the prophetic movement of the church! The church cannot clearly hear from God while paying close attention to the voice of the world. Now, before you and your social justice jargon decide to stop reading and burn these statements – read the next paragraph!

Christ was extremely clear with regards to the central law of the church – LOVE! I don't have to re-name or mask love, I don't have to call it political correctness, I don't have to call it social justice – I can simply call it love. Love should not be re-named and re-defined, because if we look around, then we will recognize that all of the counterfeit words and concepts only cover up the fact that love is still absent. We can speak using all of the politically correct etiquette, and still harbor hate. We can support social justice on the outside, and embrace social sickness internally. Love is a powerful resource that will bring forth a transformative revolution when applied through the power of the Holy Spirit. Conclusively, I do recognize the need for political correctness and social justice, outside of the context of the church – as the heathens of the world need superficial boundaries that at least present civility; even if limited within a purely academic heartless intention, but I will always maintain that true love will always supersede justice with mercy.

Where is the love?

Mark 12:29-31 And Jesus answered him, The first of all the commandments is, Hear, O Israel; The Lord our God is one Lord: And thou shalt love the Lord thy God with all thy heart, and with all thy soul, and with all thy mind, and with all thy strength: this is the first commandment. And the second is like, namely this, Thou shalt love thy neighbor as thyself. There is none other commandment greater than these.

The church should seek to love above all else, as Christ commands us to love God and our neighbor. If we love, then true political correctness and social justice will emerge. If we truly seek to analyze our social system, then we should recognize that something is tragically wrong, as churches have become involved in issues that may be important – but should not take priority over assisting the sick, poor, and spiritually starving. The church should repent for stepping over the homeless on the courthouse steps to argue secondary issues that arrest our attention away from the primary command to love. While we struggle to endorse political candidates while praying for election, weigh in on same sex issues, pontificate on pets' rights, and other issues that may need attention – people are hurting from starvation infused with conditions of abject poverty. While we debate issues and wage civil church wars within our denomination, people are dying in physical wars in foreign countries. WHERE IS THE CHURCH? WHERE IS THE LOVE! Notice that the proponents of certain issues across the country have passed referendum after referendum, yet the poor and underserved are continually ignored on a mass scale. Christ fed the hungry, cared for the sick, and restored the spiritually afflicted. Social justice makes the rich look good; love makes us all look great!

How do we say welcome?

Matthew 13:24-30 Another parable put he forth unto them, saying, The kingdom of heaven is likened unto a man which sowed good seed in his field: But while men slept, his enemy came and sowed tares among the wheat, and went his way. But when the blade was sprung up, and brought forth fruit, then appeared the tares also. So the servants of the householder came and said unto him, Sir, didst not thou sow good seed in thy field? From whence then hath it tares? He said unto them, An enemy hath done this. The servants said unto him, Wilt thou then that we go and gather them up? But he said, Nay; lest while ye gather up the tares, ye root up also the wheat with them. Let both grow together until the harvest: and in the time of harvest I will say to the reapers, Gather ye together first the tares, and bind them in bundles to burn them: but gather the wheat into my barn.

Denominations are divided over definitive components of sin, as there is growing pressure to approve or reject certain communities of people. Christ, teaching through a parable in the book of Matthew chapter 13, seem to suggest that we should allow the field to grow until the harvest. Although I was formed in the image of God I am not God; therefore I don't have the ability to harvest. If we honestly believe in the power of God, then we should embrace the work and love of Christ – that will keep us until the Lord returns. The servants questioned toward pulling up the corrupted plants, but they were instructed to leave them alone. If there were servants who did not agree with the instructions, then it seems plausible to think that they were troubled at the notion of caring for the entire field. If you let the non-corrupt and corrupt grow together, then you must nurture both plants. Our churches must continue to present love to everyone, in spite of our feelings and the thoughts that usher us to call for separation. The call for separation should take place within us, as we embrace sanctification – I can survive in the same field with the corrupted as long as my faith is anchored upon the incorruptible master of the field.

God's brand of love and not yours

Hebrews 4:12 For the word of God is quick, and powerful, and sharper than any twoedged sword, piercing even to the dividing asunder of soul and spirit, and of the joints and marrow, and is a discerner of the thoughts and intents of the heart.

Hebrews 12:1-15 Wherefore seeing we also are compassed about with so great a cloud of witnesses, let us lay aside every weight, and the sin which doth so easily beset us, and let us run with patience the race that is set before us, looking unto Jesus the author and finisher of our faith; who for the joy that was set before him endured the cross, despising the shame, and is set down at the right hand of the throne of God. For consider him that endured such contradiction of sinners against himself, lest ye be wearied and faint in your minds. Ye have not yet resisted unto blood, striving against sin. And ye have forgotten the exhortation which speaketh unto you as unto children, My son, despise not thou the chastening of the Lord, nor faint when thou art rebuked of him: For whom the Lord loveth he chasteneth, and scourgeth every son whom he receiveth. If ye endure chastening, God dealeth with you as with sons; for what son is he whom the father chasteneth not? But if ye be without chastisement, whereof all are partakers, then are ye bastards, and not sons. Furthermore we have had fathers of our flesh which corrected us, and we gave them reverence: shall we not much rather be in subjection unto the Father of spirits, and live? For they verily for a few days chastened us after their own pleasure; but he for our profit, that we might be partakers of his holiness. Now no chastening for the present seemeth to be joyous, but grievous: nevertheless afterward it yieldeth the peaceable fruit of righteousness unto them which are exercised thereby. Wherefore lift up the hands which hang down, and the feeble knees; And make straight paths for your feet, lest that which is lame be turned out of the way; but let it rather be healed. Follow peace with all men, and holiness, without which no man shall see the Lord: Looking diligently lest any man fail of the grace of God; lest any root of bitterness springing up trouble you, and thereby many be defiled;

Although love is the way of Christ, we cannot embrace a false love that lies. At times we stimulate false love with deceptive doctrine, in order to create a shallow mono-dimensional love language fused with faux feeling, hoping to satisfy our modern contextual desires. We should welcome all, but we should not lie to support superficial relationships. We should love all with the truth in the right season, as the Holy Spirit leads ministry and transformation. There have been times when I've visited children in the hospital, and it always seems to deeply disturb parents when their children have to go into surgery – yet because they love their child they almost always choose to allow doctors to operate because they believe their love will lead to life. If we withhold the truth, we have not presented the true love of God.

The truth is important, yet it should be administered under the direction of love. There is a time and a season, and there is a way to present Biblical truth toward transformative triumph in the life of the church. Love should always be the order of the day, and our ways should be flavored with the sweet peace that true love brings.

There Is Another Side

THE FATHER

And every living substance was destroyed which was upon the face of the ground, both man, and cattle, and the creeping things, and the fowl of the heaven; and they were destroyed from the earth: and Noah only remained alive, and they that were with him in the ark. Genesis 7:23

And he looked toward Sodom and Gomorrah, and toward all the land of the plain, and beheld, and, lo, the smoke of the country went up as the smoke of a furnace. Genesis 19:28

And while the flesh was yet between their teeth, ere it was chewed, the wrath of the LORD was kindled against the people, and the LORD smote the people with a very great plague. Numbers 11:33

THE SON

And when he had made a scourge of small cords, he drove them all out of the temple, and the sheep, and the oxen; and poured out the changers' money, and overthrew the tables; John 2:15

Think not that I am come to send peace on earth: I came not to send peace, but a sword. Matthew 10:34

Master, behold, the fig tree which thou cursedst is withered away. Mark 11:21

THE HOLY SPIRIT

Nevertheless I tell you the truth; It is expedient for you that I go away: for if I go not away, the Comforter will not come unto you; but if I depart, I will send him unto you. And when he is come, he will reprove the world of sin, and of righteousness, and of judgment: John 16:7-8

I have heard a great number of people (mainly non-Christians who have influenced the church to alter Biblical interpretation) define God as purely loving. Although, God is truly loving, it does not at all mean that the love is manifested in the way that it has been painted. The scriptures seem to clearly display a God of correction, that does not resemble the commercialized all-loving version of God that the church seems to advertise in the modern age. There seems to be a do what you want to do movement legitimized under that notion that God just wants everybody to be happy.

There is strong evidence throughout the Bible that God has exhibited wrathful attributes along with mercy and grace – there seems to be a point where going too far attracts detrimental consequences. There are churches that have allowed the world to define God *ex parte*, without the guidance of the scriptures and/or Holy Spirit. A false view of God is a dangerous vantage point, which is why the Bible repeatedly cautions against false prophets and teachers. We are living in an age wherein God is being re-defined to cater to congregants and our social environment. The church must advocate the truth of scripture, and renounce any movement that seeks to self-servingly destroy the integral viability of the Christian community.

Americans have drastically given up the habit of cigarette smoking, as the risk of smoking has been greatly publicized and campaigns have effectively strengthened awareness. People use to smoke because they were not fully aware of the health hazards, and the tobacco companies suppressed the fatal realities as long as they could. Some people smoked because they just did not know any better – and I would contend that some people are caught in a conundrum of transgression, because they do not know any better. Many churches are suppressing the fatal realities of sin and transgression, as they present a false depiction of God. There are great spiritual and physical health hazards joined with a do whatever you like life style, and the church is charged with issuing a continual warning!

Is anybody going to Hell?

The wicked shall be turned into hell, and all the nations that forget God. Psalms 9:17

Therefore hell hath enlarged herself, and opened her mouth without measure: and their glory, and their multitude, and their pomp, and he that rejoiceth, shall descend into it. Isaiah 5:14

And fear not them which kill the body, but are not able to kill the soul: but rather fear him which is able to destroy both soul and body in hell. Matthew 10:28

Ye serpents, ye generation of vipers, how can ye escape the damnation of hell? Matthew 23:33

And the beast was taken, and with him the false prophet that wrought miracles before him, with which he deceived them that had received the mark of the beast, and them that worshipped his image. These both were cast alive into a lake of fire burning with brimstone. Revelation 19:20

And whosoever was not found written in the book of life was cast into the lake of fire. Revelation 20:15

With all of the interpretive restructuring of the scriptures, it seems that Hell has been hard to redefine; therefore it is kept hush-hush. Ministers are rarely heard preaching sermons that acknowledge Hell, and the devil has managed to remain behind the scenes also. Preaching about Hell makes people feel uncomfortable, and if we equate transgression with consequences people will leave the congregation. Churches that embrace a standard of holiness are often talked about as being unloving. The transgressor becomes a victim to sin, and we are told by the world that we may damage them if we reference Hell. Unfortunately, people are comfortable with their sins because many ministers have failed to present the truth.

There is a story about a pastor that preached about Hell every Sunday, eventually the church fired him because they were tired of hearing about hell. The church hired a new minister, and people flocked from all around to hear him. The old ousted minister heard of the church's success and decided to visit one Sunday – to see what had changed. He was shocked to hear the new minister preaching about Hell. After worship, the old minister asked one of the prominent members, "Why do you all love your new minister so much, he is preaching about Hell also?" The member replied: "You preached as if you wanted us to go, and he preaches to save us." I fully understand that there is a proper homiletic framework that should be respected as ministers articulate the costly consequences of transgression – however, Hell cannot be completely ignored.

Additionally, it seems that the devil has been gentrified in some ways, as it seems that the eternal position of satan[5] has diminished for a more polished modern adversarial version. It seems that the devil used to be

---

[5] Intentionally left lowercase

talked about within an eternal framework, in which transgressors would spend eternal life within the devil's tormenting Hell. Now, the devil is rarely spoken of as an eternal character, a greater emphasis has been put upon satan as a pessimistic house fly kind of character – that merely disturbs day to day operations. There is a mood that the devil is an enemy that stands between me and a new car or a relationship – the devil has been painted as an obstacle between materialism and happiness. In fact the devil is a terrorist that seeks to destroy our entire future with God and we must acknowledge that satan is more than a present pipsqueak. Hell is real, the truth of the scripture should not be sequestered – but needs to be proclaimed with power, conviction, and love.

Black or White at Noon?

Romans 10:10-13 For with the heart man believeth unto righteousness; and with the mouth confession is made unto salvation. For the scripture saith, Whosoever believeth on him shall not be ashamed. For there is no difference between the Jew and the Greek: for the same Lord over all is rich unto all that call upon him. For whosoever shall call upon the name of the Lord shall be saved.

There are a great number of congregants that embrace the notion that race is no longer a factor within our society. Although there are a greater number of integrated/multi-cultural congregations – we are still far from a universally integrated church. Some denominations are equally multiracial, yet individual congregations remain un-integrated. If one looks around church on Sunday at noon, it seems that separation continues to reside within the church. Many churches have never even worshiped with another congregation of a predominantly different race. Schools are integrated, the workplace is integrated, bars are integrated – it would seem that the church should be integrated (I'm just saying).

Icons

Deuteronomy 12:32 What thing soever I command you, observe to do it: thou shalt not add thereto, nor diminish from it.

Revelation 22:18-19 For I testify unto every man that heareth the words of the prophecy of this book, If any man shall add unto these things, God shall add unto him the plagues that are written in this book: And if any man shall take away from

the words of the book of this prophecy, God shall
take away his part out of the book of life, and out
of the holy city, and from the things which are
written in this book.

The canonization of the Bible refers to the way in which it is structured, in terms of the placement of chapters and books. The Hebrew Bible and the Christian Bible contain the same words; however, the books appear in different orders. The Christian Bible is organized in relation to two testaments or divisions, whereas the Hebrew Bible is structured within a reality that awaits a messiah.

When we think in Biblical terms we must consider reality as a paramount function of our systematized beliefs. It is my understanding of life that we all live within the context of a certain reality. I would argue that all reality is culturally interpreted - whereas many scholars would vehemently oppose. The world of academia does not sincerely embrace cultural relativism because like most systemic institutions the germ of racism infects the organism, and causes the knowledge to emerge with consistent deformities. Cultural relative reality seems best as it is difficult for us to arrive at any test of concrete reality without first consulting our "Mother" – culture!

Your mother may have abandoned you upon the doorsteps of time – however, if you are alive today – she produced you through some amount of incubation time. Therefore you spent time in the water-filled mountain and your first experiences were transferred through mother to you! Many people who do not believe and/or read the Bible, embrace theories that derive from an anti-cultural manifestation of racist culture – the icons of lies called truth.

The Bible was canonized by fools under the influence of a powerful God – some of the world's biggest dummies put the Bible in order in terms of man power. I have lots of reasons for saying that they were crazy, primarily because the Western, or at the time Northern world did not understand the principles of peace, love, joy, harmony, happiness, reciprocity, and divinity. However, we can examine the existential reality and understand that systems of class, caste, and race were almost innate within the Northern peoples. The translation, transliteration, canonization, and publication of the Bible was the biggest mistake of the Northern world (I will refer to the western world as northern, because within historical and scientific analysis we know that Africa is the mother continent).

The last several hundred years have been based upon trying to reverse the tides of truth within the Bible – the first approach of the Northern world was to iconize the Bible by painting pictures of the deity and Biblical

117

characterizations within the context of their own phenotypic scope, while attempting to pronounce themselves episcopal. The problem with the icons or the comic book Bible approach is that the text of the Torah (first five books of the Hebrew Bible) and first division of the Christian Bible – concretely characterize African people and beyond the characterization is the fact the Bible clearly states many locations and families that are irreversibly connected to Africa.

It is fully clear to me that had I been from the Northern culture it would have been to my best interest to destroy the Bible – but the God of power did not allow such destruction to the eternal culture of the African people. The Northerners had a burning desire to have a God – throughout the history of the Northern culture; from cave to cave we do not find any conclusive evidence of a systematized structure of deified proportions. The man without a God thirsted for the intrinsic power that can only radiate from the connection of deity and anthropology, therefore in a feeble attempt to embrace God the Northerners perpetrated a fraud and subsequently stole the African's image of God, leaving nothing but fingerprints and the Bible.

We can research volumes of Northern (*Western*) rhetoric, and the idealism of deified structures does not seem to emerge from the hieroglyphic text of any Northern (*Western*) cave. People must now know the truth, the door has been opened – and the captives will be set free. We have been taught to read the Bible in part, so that the full impartation of the word could not be felt among the people. We must begin to read the Bible from the first page to the last.

The Bible is the story of an African family leading nations, toward one God (from polytheism to monotheism). If race does not matter, as I often hear from the White culture, then it should be easy to embrace the truth. Although we cannot paint a physical portrait of God we should recognize that Abraham along with the founding fathers of our religion was dark, and information strongly suggests that Christ was dark or at the very least brown. If race does not matter, then why do many Whites still insist on portraying Christ as White with blue eyes and blond hair? I'm even willing to give up the notion of normalizing a portrait of Christ with dark skin and dreadlocks, if White people would give up their portraits. If we agree that we don't honestly know what Christ looks like – let us also agree not to be offensive and force a more than likely inaccurate image upon the world.

A Voice From The South says: "There is an old proverb 'The devil is always painted black – by White painters.' And what is needed, perhaps, to reverse the picture of the lordly man slaying the lion, is for the lion to turn painter"[6].

---

[6] Cooper, Anna J. A Voice From The South. New York: Oxford University Press, 1988. (P.225)

Betrayed, bewildered, and blessed

It seems to me that many of our present struggles stem from a misrepresentation of the past through the process of recorded history. Many accounts of history present the notion that Europeans held the belief that Africa was a heathen nation, although the Hebrew and Christian Bibles contain evidence that many key Biblical events took place upon the African continent. Scientific research continues to lead institutional knowledge toward Africa, in relation to the creation of man and notions of religion. The concept of polytheism and monotheism both emerged from the continent of Africa - however, the modern era seems to strip the locations away from Biblical events, continuing to say that the origin of worshippers is not as relevant as the system of worship. There seems to be a preference toward classifying Biblical people as Hebrew, Israelite, and/or Jewish - without any reference to African. Universities and colleges often place Biblical studies within

121

departments of Eastern and Near Eastern cultures – while African studies feature voodoo.

The reality of Africa within the Holy Scriptures becomes important to the metaphysical reality of African-Americans, as the people began to examine the image of God from whom man was created. In order to enslave the total African personality, the first step was the theft and distortion of the African concept of reality, as created by theological perceptions at the core of ancient African life. The continual suppression of Biblical facts seems to weaken the primary perspective upon which theological concepts are often built. Our collective view of God must begin with the truth in order to gain the most complete view of the Creator.

Segregation and religion, fought fear

During the period of slavery one of the most important catalysts toward freedom was the ability to assemble within an institutional systematized structure. In order to keep the slaves under subjection, it was necessarily important to make them incapable of carrying out mass systems of communication. However the barbaric civility of White America contained a method to the utter madness created by slavery, therefore moral pressures persisted in favor of religiously educating slaves. Early on there was divisive strife surrounding the creation of the Black Church from both internal and external forces.

The first Negro Baptist Church was founded by Andrew Bryan during the period of American slavery in Georgia. Andrew Bryan and a number of slaves were persecuted by Whites for gathering for church activities; as there was a fear of insurrection. It is more than strange that Europeans enslaved people of color because they were perceived to be godless savages, and when the Africans attempted to worship, they were prohibited. The task of missionaries and enslavers was to direct Africans toward reform from their perceived wicked and heathenish ways, yet when Africans sought to worship – White fear ruled the day. Remnants of this fear continue to persist within denominations; therefore we must be acutely aware of the foundational issues. It seems that if the church allows society to dictate the doctrine of the church, we will continually arrive at similar systems that defy the central tenet of love. Thankfully, over time many Whites became sympathetic and possibly ashamed of the esthetics of disallowing slaves to worship, therefore many slaves were allowed to worship in large log cabins on Sundays, with a White overseer present. I would argue that political correctness and social justice are euphemistic ancestors of an esthetic movement, which should have been motivated by the love of Christ.

Slaves were prohibited from learning to read English, therefore slave preachers were often permitted to attend White churches in order to gain sermonic perspective from the White preacher. Historically there was a paranoia embraced by Whites in response toward black assembly and mass communication. Skepticism looms above race centered churches as a result of the historically dysfunctional relationship between American churches and denominations. Although it seems that the society has grown, remnants of the past seem to remain, as churches are still largely racially segregated.

Although segregated worship helped to form a system of segregated churches, it was also the morality of various Whites that aided Black people toward stability within the organization of the Black church. The Methodist denomination for one believed that Negroes should be free and have opportunities for learning. Education gave Blacks opportunities to emerge as scholars and leaders within the Black church community, and Whites who sought the education of Blacks indirectly sought the liberation and freedom of Black people.

It seems that in order for liberation to take place within any group, a strong social and communication system must first emerge, and it appears that the modern church must embrace an inclusive system of learning. Whites and Blacks should share in the creation and presentation of curriculum in seminaries, as holistic faith; this requires a gestaltist academic paradigm. The church must institutionally place church history within the proper contextual framework; that may allow us to obtain a platform from which to view the modern church in order to preserve optimal systems of socio-theological metaphysical transcendental homogeneity.

The pre-modern Black church under dim light

Throughout the late 19th century the Black educated elite often over generalized indigenous African religion, as they gleaned from a Western body of knowledge that caused them to illustrate African religion in a negative tone. Therefore, I believe that both Blacks and Whites are responsible for the suppression of church history. Many Whites are historically responsible for the foundation of ignorance that catapulted systematized suppression, and many Blacks continue to unquestionably build upon suboptimal systems of suppression.

I stated earlier that American slave preachers were educated by White preachers. Unfortunately, the preacher was one of the key instruments used by Whites to spread distorted ideologies to Negros, mixed with falsehoods containing imagery of a White savior named Jesus. The practice of serving and worshiping a White image conveyed the superiority of White people.

The Negro's environment was mostly staged by the White power structure, cast by educators and preachers indoctrinated with Whites' version of the truth. The implementation of White religious ideology was an attempt to totally control the Black man's intrinsic structure. Imprisonment, chains, and mutilation could only control the physical body, and numerous lynchings would destroy the American work force. For maximum service the best alternative was to control the intrinsic mechanism of Black people. Controlling one's religion is an easy way to largely control one's thinking.

The initial structure of the Black church was primarily subject to the White power structure, and resembled the White American church. Negroes were intravenously fed Christianity by transliterating Whites that professed to be missionaries. In all actuality they were proselytizing fabricators who robbed Negroes of true indigenous theology, Christianity, and religion, while attempting to control Black theological voice and thought. White churches and Black churches are inextricably connected, and although I realize that both races are often resistant to inclusive denominational relationships – I don't think Heaven will be segregated. It is time to include and embrace the truth, which will help us heal the church and nation.

Africans were illustrated as having the wrong religion and therefore heathen. Socio-theological agency was destroyed, Africa was stripped of divine rite as righteous, and Africans were treated like helpless children all on the basis of religion. Pope Alexander VI issued the following statement:

"Among other works well pleasing to divine majesty and cherished of our heart, this assuredly ranks highest, that in our times especially the Catholic faith and the Christian religion be exalted and everywhere increased and spread, that the health of souls be cared for and that barbarous nations be overthrown and brought to faith itself."

The primary reasoning which perpetuated the enslavement and disenfranchisement of Africans was built upon systems of religious political power. If the American church remains segregated, what synergizes our theological perspective and prevents future domination based upon individualized ideology? The church must collectively articulate the motivating voice, urging divine and socio-theological consciousness. The church should embrace a Biblical ideology seeking to capture the purist interpretation without the chains of racism; additionally the recent past should not be hidden from the church history narrative.

While we are on the subject – African religion is often oversimplified and portrayed as ontologically savage because of animal sacrifice, when the Jewish Torah and Christian Bibles contain explicit details of animal sacrifice – and human sacrifice - as it is to my understanding that the hero of the Christian Bible died on a cross for atonement.

It seems to me that the church along with scholars of theology must continue to define theology from the perspective of the believer in order to formulate an optimal ministerial foundation. In the past and present, the African-American experience has been often overlooked – as Black Theology, as a divination of liberation, and cannot be properly examined without the necessary components of socio-political metaphysical transcendental theological reality formed through the process of divine bilateral acculturation as processed upon the ancestral frontier of Africa and the recent passage of the Americas and oppressing western cultural trauma of the middle passage, and sub-optimal conditioning experienced for more than two centuries. We have come a long way, yet we have a long way to go before we reach Mt. Zion.

The Pastor

In the Bible, God is quoted: "I will give you pastors according to mine heart, which shall feed you with knowledge and understanding. (Jeremiah 3:15)" Pastors are an important component to the life of the church as God has ordained them. Biblically, historically, and doctrinally the pastor is the leader, administrator, and overseer within the Baptist Church. This article will attempt to define the office of pastor in relation to the church and the spiritually systematized structure of leadership within the parish fold.

Leadership has been important to God from the very beginning, as Adam was appointed by God to guide life in the Garden - and later he was made responsible for Eve. Adam was the prophet, priest, and king of the Garden - he was the first spiritual leader and pastor. The father was God's first conduit toward spiritual authority. We may observe the leadership of men like Noah, Abraham, Isaac, and Jacob – these founders of our faith began their ministries with the familiarity of family.

Abraham is the most prominent within the fathers of our faith, as we are able to find a plethora of passages that depict his leadership. The Bible says:

> *And they came to the place which God had told him of; and Abraham built an altar there, and laid the wood in order, and bound Isaac his son, and laid him on the altar upon the wood (Genesis 22:9).*

Abraham illustrates the ministry of leadership as he follows God's instruction, built an altar (a place to worship God), and led his son to become bound within divine instructions. Abraham does not overly explain his action nor does Isaac become overly inquisitive, it seems that Isaac's willingness presents his trust in the God of his father. How many of us would be willing to surrender to

God's power manifested through the man of God? I've heard people say any number of times that they would only be moved, only if God spoke to them personally – in most cases the word of the Lord has been delivered through the man of God. In the Bible, Romans chapter 10 expounds that preachers help us to gain faith through the proclamation of the Gospel. It seems that Abraham not only led Isaac to the physical altar, but he led him to the only wise God – as Isaac followed the same God and led his children toward the presence of the eternal God of Abraham.

Time moves on and people change, yet God remains the same and leadership continued to be important within the process of the emergence of our faith. Families began to multiply and migrate, the Bible focuses on Jacob's (Israel) family which numerically grew in spite of enslavement in Egypt. God ordained their freedom using Moses as the primary vehicle to facilitate the liberation of the Israelite family. Moses became the unilateral leader chosen by God to lead the people. When the Israelites departed from Egypt they were more than just a family; they were a mixed multitude. Not long after the Israelites crossed the Red Sea out of Egypt the Lord commanded Moses to establish the priesthood.

> *And thou shalt bring Aaron and his sons unto the door of the tabernacle of the congregation and wash them with water. And thou shalt put upon Aaron holy garments, and anoint him, and sanctify him; that he may minister unto me in the priest's office. (Exodus 40:12-13)*

The priesthood established during the Mosaic Era constitutes the foundation perpetuating our current system of leadership, worship, and liturgy.

The tradition of the New Testament Bible records in Thessalonians 5:12-13, "But we beseech you, brethren, to respect those who labor among you, and are over you in the Lord and admonish you, and to esteem them very highly in love because of their work." The key phrase is "and are over you in the Lord." The Greek word is *prohistamenous*, translated "over you" in the King James version. The pastor serves the congregation as the leader – not as a boss, but as the messenger of the Lord - and the Word of God should compel us to follow the instructions proclaimed by the man of God. The pastor is an overseer, leading the people in the way that God has commanded.

The office of pastor is supported in Hebrews 13:17, urging us to follow leadership ("Obey your leaders and submit to them, for they are keeping watch over your souls, as men who will have to give account"). The imperative translated "obey" emerges from the word *peitho*, "to persuade." Congregants must be pliable to the persuasion teaching of the Bible through Holy Spirit led preaching and teaching. This further illustrated the fact that just as the account of Abraham and Isaac willingly followed the instructions of God, we must be willing to be led by those whom God has placed before us as vessels.

In the New Testament, and by Christian writers to the end of the second century, ministers are called by the function they perform: Overseer (Episkipos), Elder (Presbuteros), Minister (Diakonos). "There were no levels of office in the apostolic age. Character, gifts and responsibility were the only ground of distinction." Pastor, Teacher, Presbyter (Elder) and Bishop (Overseer) are one and the same office in the New Testament, according to Calvin, Luther, and Wycliffe. Many church fathers can be cited with regard to the only offices being that of deacon and elder. According to the *Hiscox Guide for Baptist Churches and the Baptist Tradition*, within the context of the Baptist Church the offices of pastor and deacon are the only universally recognized ecclesiastic offices.

We have the example of the Ephesians elders – "From Miletus, Paul sent to Ephesus for the elders of the church." (Acts 20:17) "Keep watch over yourselves and all the flock of which the Holy Spirit has made you overseers. Be shepherds of the church of God, which he bought with his own blood." (Acts 20:28). Note all three titles are used for the same leaders. The Baptist Church applies all ecclesiastic titles to the one office of pastor – for example, pastors follow the guidelines for bishops, elders, and/or apostles etc. However there are exceptions to the interchangeability of these terms and titles.

The pastor's authority comes from God, and it becomes the congregation's responsibility to follow the leadership that God has ordained. Gifts for leadership are not from man (political), but from God (Galatians 1:16-17). The early church apostles had authority based on their personal contact with Jesus. "When they saw the courage of Peter and John and realized that they were unschooled,

139

ordinary men, they were astonished and they took note that these men had been with Jesus (Acts 4:13)."

>*"I tell you the truth, whatever you bind on earth will be bound in heaven, and whatever you loose on earth will be loosed in heaven (Matthew 18:18)."*

The Man of God has great spiritual and physical authority, because it is the responsibility of the pastor to lead the flock in the direction that God mandates. "It was he who gave some to be apostles, some to be prophets, some to be evangelists, and some to be pastors and teachers, to prepare God's people for works of service, so that the body of Christ may be built up (Ephesians 4:11-12). In the Corinthian instruction: "And in the church, God had appointed first of all apostles, second prophets, third teachers, then workers of miracles, also those having gifts of healing, those able to help others, those with gifts of administration, and those speaking in different kinds of tongues (I Cor. 12:28)." However, the evolution of the Baptist Church based upon Mathew 18:18 has formed the basic doctrine that the pastor is the overseer and leader of every facet of church ministry.

This is why prayer, fasting, and awareness of the Spirit's guidance is an integral part of leadership acceptance.

> *"They all joined together constantly in prayer, along with the women and Mary the mother of Jesus, and with his brothers. Then they prayed, 'Lord, you know everyone's heart. Show us which of these two you have chosen to take over this apostolic ministry, which Judas left to go where he belongs.' Then they cast lots, and the lot fell to Matthias; so he was added to the eleven apostles." (Acts 1:14, 24-26)*

141

"While they were worshipping the Lord and fasting, the Holy Spirit said, 'Set apart for me Barnabas and Saul for the work to which I have called them.' So after they had fasted and prayed, they placed their hands on them and sent them off (Acts 13:2-3)."

"Paul and Barnabas appointed elders for them in each church and, with prayer and fasting, committed them to the Lord, in whom they had put their trust (Acts 14:23)."

This is why it is more than imperative that the church stay in connection with God when awaiting the appointment of a pastor – as the Lord will provide our every need, we only need to be receptive of Holy guidance.

God-called pastors (the same office is called elder and bishop) to have authority over the assemblies (Acts 20:28; 1 Th. 5:12; Ph. 1:1; 1 Tim. 3:1; Tit. 1:7). Church congregations come under God's authority through the vehicle of the pastoral office. The church does not submit to man, but to the Chief Shepherd through the under shepherd – the pastor. Abuses of pastoral authority do not negate the fact that the Bible tells us that God has given authority to pastors and do not negate the fact that the Bible demands that we submit to God-called pastors. Even in cases in which a Christian has been under the influence of an abusive or unscriptural pastoral situation, he or she must maintain a proper spirit and attitude in regard to pastoral authority. He should leave such a church, if necessary, and find a spiritually healthy church, which is led by a God-called man, and join it and submit to their God-given authority. A Christian must carefully guard his spirit so that he does not become bitter. He must examine himself before the Lord to be sure that he is not rebellious toward genuine God-given authority. Sometimes we think the problem is with those who have the rule over us when in reality it is with our own stubborn spirits.

Testimony

I have arrived at the thought that future generations may need to understand parts of my testimony, with special thought toward future pastors. I was born into a Christian family, and was subsequently baptized when I was six or seven years old – on the same day with a man who would later become the deacon board chair, and chief deacon that would call for my resignation from the office of pastor thirty years after our baptism.

I've been uniquely shaped as a Christian, I grew up in a Christian family – that seemed to live as Christians better than most of the people I knew. Both my maternal and paternal grandmothers were fairly strong Christians. My maternal grandmother took me to church even when my parents didn't go; however, both of my parents attended church on a regular basis up until my father became turned off by the church because of an issue with

145

family and integrity. I have a lot of love for my family; although I share my father's disdain for people who toy with the church and embrace hypocritical lifestyles. Certainly pastors, ministers, and deacons should guard their lifestyles through the power of the Holy Spirit. Before I arrived at the full knowledge of what disgusted my father, I was often misled to think that the issues were abstract extremist constructions that did not necessitate his acute response. In stark contrast to my father's way, my reaction to satanic agents within the church has been to resist the temptation to become isolated, and boldly embrace God's word and power through the Holy Spirit. Rather than abandon the church, it seems to me that one voice of truth is stronger at a whisper than a thousand amplified lies.

Although my parents did not always attend church during my father's revolt – my grandmother took me to a Baptist church practically every Sunday with the exception of a few Sundays that I would attend church with my maternal grandfather, who belonged to an African Methodist Episcopal Zion church. I liked going to church with my grandfather (the only time I enjoyed him, as he was always peaceful at church) because the Methodists never worshiped over an hour and a half. The church was also very beautiful, although you could tell that there was an atmosphere of sophistication. My grandfather was bald, but he would even wear a wig to church; joining in the grand African Methodist parade of professionals. The Methodist church had an educated minister in stark contrast to our Baptist church wherein our minister could only read the Bible. His limited education did not seem to hinder his preaching, as well as I remember - but the church membership seemed primitively Southern. The Methodists had books (hymn books and pew Bibles) - whereas the Baptists sang songs emerging from a tradition of memory and made up extemporaneous emotions set to a fast or slow meter.

147

The Baptist church was much more soulful than the Methodist, and the Baptist music was often very motivating – people would shout and dance so much that the church was sometimes referred to as Holy Ghost headquarters (traditionally people believed that shouting was the primary effect of the Holy Spirit). The Baptist church was packed with people almost every Sunday, although it wasn't a big building – yet at the time it seemed large enough. There were about seventy to one hundred members, and back then that was great for a church building built in the 1950s by the pastor and a few men of the church, after having founded the church in a storefront that they were forced to leave because of highway construction.

I was brought up in an environment where I was able to see more than most. I experienced both sides of African American church life; the soulful and the sophisticated were always before me. Along with that I attended Catholic school through the second grade; I attended mass every Wednesday – I had to learn all of the prayers and customs; early on the Catholics gave me a strong dislike for school! I enjoyed mass (except for all the kneeling) – but at all other times the Catholics were just plain mean. The experience of Catholic school would cause me to be suspect of White culture for many years, because all of my instructors were White.

Finally, I was shaped by my grandmother's love of Biblically Hebrew customs – my family had a great understanding of the Bible; as they studied often. My grandmother had worked for a Rabbi and her mother had worked for Zionists (sometimes referred to as Jews) also. My surname was a result of the Byrd family selling my great-great grandfather (West Indian) to a Jewish family with the Americanized name Shaw[7]. Because many of the

---

[7] Americanization of a similar sounding Ashkenazic Jewish surname

Jewish customs are detailed within the Bible my maternal grandmother taught me to practice some of the Hebrew customs, which strengthened my devotion to the way of the Bible. Later the things that she taught me would provide the road that I would need to keep me devoted to the Christian faith. So many experiences have shaped my world view through the scope of the Christian faith.

My family was not perfect, we had some issues – but I don't remember them to be extreme. My mother was a strong praying woman that was oftentimes thought to be anti-social because she did not get involved in the young party culture of the early 1970s. She had a temper, which she struggled with through prayer for many years. My father was very mild mannered and quiet – however when he spoke it was always in parables and riddles steeped in some philosophical armchair tradition articulated in broken English seasoned with a posh, polished, proper, pontifical accent.

The first few years of my education were depressing, as my parents insisted upon a Catholic school. Eventually I was able to persuade them to release me from the prison of terror into the public school system. After transferring to public school, life was easier – although the Catholics thought I was dumb, I was far ahead of many public school children; so they put me in a gifted class. While there was great potential for me, I never regained a love for school or trust for White folks until after high school – therefore I was never more than an average student, who hated school and everything that was associated with the same. I didn't like teachers; because most (all but two from grades three through twelve) were White – additionally I did not like my classmates either, because my family culture was so different from the average familial social construction within my environment. We lived in the ghetto (for Columbus), but my grandparents strived to show me a different life – so we traveled, we stayed in the best hotels, toured many places, and ate the best foods.

Morally, we lived by a different standard – Sunday was sacred and holy, no playing! My bicycle was locked up all day on Sunday – we went to church, then came home and had more church with a bucket of Kentucky Fried Chicken. My grandmother always had a piano, and after church – we would sing, talk about church, and study the Bible. My grandmother would also host Bibles study groups at her home – there were times when a Bible study would just organically start when people would visit.

I had a personal encounter with God, and started preaching at the age of twelve – needless to say, a church-boy did not always fit in so well within the public school tapestry – so much so that when I was a sophomore in high school I begged to be released early, threatening to drop out. My high school counselor arranged for my early graduation – therefore I went to summer school and skipped junior year. During my high school years, I was blessed to have to opportunity to connect with a community of young Christians (thirty to fifty students); we prayed collectively before homeroom every morning, and gathered for Bible study weekly after school.

Many disappointments and an era of great depression would emerge not long after high school. My father died when I was 15, although he remained faithful to God, he never regularly returned to church with the exception of a few times he came to hear me preach and his funeral. My grandparents did not get along well and often remained at odds with each other. I spent a lot of time with my grandmother; and it always seemed that my grandfather was somehow jealous of our relationship – therefore, I did not have a real male figure with the exception of my pastor, during my high school years.

Once I received a driver's license I started attending a Baptist church of my choice that seemed to be a combination of the soulfulness and structured sophistication worship styles that I had become accustomed to during the dichotomy of worship that infused my childhood. I loved my pastor, because he had the integrity that many other ministers seemed to lack at the time. The church members were more than kind, and they embraced me with an endearing love.

After high school I wanted to go to Morehouse College in Atlanta, Georgia – where I had been accepted; but the tuition prohibited me from going. I was given the opportunity to work with the Billy Graham Evangelistic Association, so for two years after high school I traveled and focused on evangelism – learning everything I could. Subsequently, my grandmother enrolled me in barber college which I did not like. I left and enrolled in Shaw University (Raleigh, NC) however, because of overcrowding I did not stay – I returned to Ohio and enrolled in The Ohio State University. School was great for me, I enjoyed being a campus man – and I found out that I was smart. For the first time in my life I felt a sense of accomplishment. I could write, think, and trade ideas with scholars – the process of academia was more than fascinating for me. Additionally, somewhere between meeting White people within the Billy Graham Association and on campus – I learned to appreciate their culture, releasing the bitterness of my Catholic school experience.

I preached for a rural church in Southern Ohio outside of Cincinnati for a few months, and was subsequently called to the office of pastor. The church had been founded in 1843 by manumitted slaves that had come from Virginia. The town was filled with racist undertones and the people were ruggedly skeptical of everybody and everything. I lived with my maternal grandparents and commuted to the church on alternating Sundays – the church was 80 miles outside of Columbus. I preached on the first and third Sunday of each month and preached for a variety of other churches on the alternate Sundays from Easter to Thanksgiving (the rural church had a winter sabbatical each year from Thanksgiving to Easter), which helped to supplement my otherwise meager income.

The arrangement with the church provided that I be given half of whatever the general offering was on the weeks that I was present; for the first few years I would take home between $6.00 and $25.00 – I remained the pastor for 14 years. The community did not grow and although attendance was consistent, there were rarely new people. The church did not decline through death, yet illness was a factor that claimed a few from time to time, which kept them away for several weeks. There were only two funerals during the time that I served as pastor, as the Lord blessed us not to lose members from an already strained membership. It seems to me that the people were extremely hard to get along with! But as I think about things, I may have been part of the problem. My personality has often been described as arrogant, abrasive, evasive, elitist, and academically tempered, yet I tend to think that my firm convictions in the faith, joined with integrity for ministry, causes the unfaithful to call me names. Beyond all of that, I have been taught to tell the truth, and the average person cannot deal with honesty. Over the years my personality has softened with the lessons of fatherhood. Our children often help us to see ourselves, and in turn we become better people.

The church invited me to resign within the first month of my pastorate – I asked for keys to the building and they refused to give me keys. They said that if I had keys it would increase the budget, if I used my office – the water bill would increase, paper towels, coffee, electric, and etc. They told me that if I needed access to the building they would let me in; and if I insisted on keys, I could just leave. WOW! I agreed to leave just like I came –

I told them that a council of churches came to ordain and install me, and I would call a council to mediate the issue before offering my resignation. I gave them 30 days to give me keys or I would call a council of churches. They gave me keys on the thirty-first day after the disagreement. I have always heard pastors talk about the honeymoon period; however, I have never witnessed a honeymoon period. The second church I was called to did not provide me with an initial blissful period either; several congregants called for my resignation less than a year after I had been installed as pastor.

There have been times where my age has been held against me, whereby older members have resisted my leadership. During my first experience as a pastor, the rural congregants called me junior for the first three years of my service. Many of them did not acknowledge me as pastor until after the Lord used me to get a clear deed to the church property. The church had worshiped on the same land since 1843, interestingly enough during the early years two congregations (one Baptist, and the other Methodist) worshiped on the same land using alternating Sundays. Slaves had been given the land for worship; however in 1947 a White man sold the land to a railroad company without any prior deed. The only right the church had to the land was a covenant recorded in the county courthouse that provided a place of worship with some restrictions. I partnered with a friend (graduate student) from the university and a professor from the history department to research the church history. It was an interesting adventure that led to information from the 1700's. We compiled a history book that I later presented to the railroad company, demanding a clear deed without a covenant relationship – the title was released a few months later (I had finally become pastor). The church was a great blessing as I gained many experiences.

During my service within the rural community, I was called to serve another congregation with another minister. After two years of service I was selected to pastor the urban church full time. There were a number of issues that presented themselves coming in the door, and not long after my installation – I was being asked to resign. Requests to resign seem to be the perpetual story of my life, therefore this was merely a different song with the same refrain. I tend to think that people first became upset when I encouraged the restructuring of the spending and accounting process. It seemed to me that there were some issues whereby money was being collected in the name of the church, but never made it to the church. There was also money being collected and placed into separate treasuries that were unaccounted for, and we developed a system that demanded accountability. Oddly enough, some of the people who elected to migrate to other congregations are actively raising money in their new places of worship. Second, I accepted and supported recommendations from the church trustees to liquidate the transportation service, as it had become more of a liability than a valued resource for ministry. Third, I requested that people call me before dropping by to visit my home. Fourth, I supported the ordination of women deacons, and inclusion on the all-male ministry board. Finally, I recommended that the church change locations based upon a God-given vision.

The recommendation to move was the straw that broke the camel's back – all hell broke loose! Although there was a great season of unrest, with mean letters being forwarded bearing the names of people I grew up around – the Holy Spirit continued to provide me with the wisdom to keep the saints praying and not fighting. There was never a fight, because it takes two for a fight! The officers and supporters of leadership were instructed not to say a defensive word; just let the pastor deal with the disgruntled members (sheep should never fight other sheep or goats). People came out to meetings who had not attended church in years; the chairman of the deacon board led the movement to fire me (he was baptized in the same water on the same day that I was in the 1970s). Other issues re-emerged as I could see and feel the barrier that deterred my father years prior, dealing with family members.

Through a season of midnight, the Lord continually kept me strong – after nearly a year of turmoil, the church moved. The Lord pruned the congregation and a number of members did not remain a part of the congregation, however the Lord immeasurably blessed the remnant that moved. I have come to learn over the years conflict will come; however, all we must do is stay connected to God through the Holy Spirit – if the Lord places us in a position, we cannot afford to be fearful; if we do as God leads, then everything will work out for the good.

Different

Now therefore, if ye will obey my voice indeed, and keep my covenant, then ye shall be a peculiar treasure unto me above all people: for all the earth is mine: (Exodus 19:5)

But ye are a chosen generation, a royal priesthood, an holy nation, a peculiar people; that ye should shew forth the praises of him who hath called you out of darkness into his marvelous light: (1 Peter 2:9)

The scriptures teach us that the people of God should be different from everybody else. There are outside forces that have always challenged the authority of the church as a vessel for truth. I have heard Christians waver from God's truth based on worldly personalities imposing the thought that accuracy comes through the conformation of multitudes. Although there seems to be viability in the theory of universality – we must not forget that our omnipresent God continues to maintain individually unique relationships congruent with the collective community of God.

Noah[8] and his family were singled out as upright in the midst of unrighteous peoples, Lot[9] and his family were spared (partly upon the covenant of Abraham) from the wrath of God in a wicked land, and remnants of Israel[10] along with a variety of other separated individuals have been found pleasing to God in spite of antithetical actions by multitudes. The Bible tends to suggest that courage, heroism, and valor often emerge from a person or small group of people who dare to be different from normative Neanderthals. The church, in an effort to become aligned with the mainstream of society under the intoxicating

---

[8] Genesis 7:1
[9] Genesis 19:29
[10] Jeremiah 23:3

influence of materialism, seems to want to assimilate into the modern culture as an affirming complex rather than an aspiring community that seeks to please God. The worldly forces of evil will continually attempt to entice the church toward the broad way that leads to destruction.

The church is challenged to remain content even in the midst of lonely seasons. It has often been said that the road to perdition is paved with good intentions, although we cannot concretely affirm how the road is paved – we do know that the road to destruction is wide, and narrow is the way that leads to life which few will find. The church must learn to often stand alone, through the megaphone magnified voices of devilish dissenting disciples.

Put the stones away; a boulder is headed your way

Disrespectful comments toward clergy often emerge from the way that many clergy continue to display reckless lifestyles (if the shoes fit, wear them or go barefoot). Additionally, many younger clergy have been selected and promoted through denominational political systematized régimes. We live in an age where greed and prestige attempt to capture the bride of Christ, and the harlot often neglects her groom for the deadly trinity (lust of: the flesh, the eye, and the pride of life[11]). The ministry mafia comprised of denominational powerbrokers often place church leaders based on superficial status – from showmanship to societal success factors that are most often antithetical to spiritually Biblical foundations.

We should remain prayerful for accused ministers – as there may be more demons lurking in the margins of

---

[11] 1John 2:16

their chapters; the church and clergy must be careful not to give allegation the kind of attention that may breed copycat accusations (true and false) against ministers in pulpits across the county. When this litigious society gets an idea, they will run with it to courthouses throughout the states to extort money and power from the church. Jesting jousting jackleg ministers are a great stain on the church; however, the church must deal with them carefully, as a carnival can easily be transformed into a circus. We must be careful: a mess anywhere is a mess everywhere and can potentially devastate all of our churches. Some denominations have had great difficulty recovering from accusations of sexual misconduct, some statements may be true and others are false – although many denominations *episcopally* join churches; sexual malfeasance surely has not taken place in every individual church – but every church suffers from what happened in a few.

Our best defenses are prayer, silence, and neutrality –
until God moves us toward action. Additionally, some of
us can't afford to get involved with foolishness as in some
denominational circles; there are only a few recognized
sins because sexual preferences are not factors.
Homosexuality is accepted, along with polygamy
depending on where you worship. Many of our
denominations (mine included) can't completely focus on
ministry, because we've continued to waste time on sexual
issues – while in the backdrop of our cathedrals the world
is in desperate need of Christ's salvific power through the
ministry of the Gospel!

COMMUNION

The great reset movement of the church

1 Corinthians 11:23-34 For I have received of the Lord that which also I delivered unto you, That the Lord Jesus the same night in which he was betrayed took bread: And when he had given thanks, he brake it, and said, Take, eat: this is my body, which is broken for you: this do in remembrance of me. After the same manner also he took the cup, when he had supped, saying, This cup is the new testament in my blood: this do ye, as oft as ye drink it, in remembrance of me. For as often as ye eat this bread, and drink this cup, ye do shew the Lord's death till he come. Wherefore whosoever shall eat this bread, and drink this cup of the Lord, unworthily, shall be guilty of the body and blood of the Lord. But let a man examine himself, and so let him eat of that bread, and drink of that cup. For he that eateth and drinketh unworthily, eateth and

169

drinketh damnation to himself, not discerning the Lord's body. For this cause many are weak and sickly among you, and many sleep. For if we would judge ourselves, we should not be judged. But when we are judged, we are chastened of the Lord, that we should not be condemned with the world. Wherefore, my brethren, when ye come together to eat, tarry one for another. And if any man hunger, let him eat at home; that ye come not together unto condemnation. And the rest will I set in order when I come.

With all of the distractions that come with life, it becomes easy to forget things; our memories are often overloaded by a multiplex of media outputs along with demanding occupations. If we are honest, it's easy to forget and it has nothing to do with age as it did in generations past – now the young and the old have trouble remembering. The church may forget from time to time the main focus, side-tracked by a variety of mundane pressures – however, Communion should reset our memories. Even with the magnificence of the modern computer, every now and then they freeze or become sluggish, demanding a re-boot. Christ instructed the disciples to observe Communion, and remember Him.

No matter what the church is going through, and no matter how far we have strayed from the presence and purpose of God, Communion should remind us to come back. We should come to the Communion table having examined ourselves through the guidance of the Holy Spirit. The church should embrace the memory of Christ, as he bled, suffered, died, and arose that we may grip the greatness of salvation. Oh, when we think of the goodness of Jesus, and all that He has done for us – our collective soul should shout with hallelujah praise! The church cannot earnestly participate in Communion, and remain dysfunctional from a business session, or wearied with worldly woes. Congregations must be taught to respect the importance and sanctity of Communion, and then given the resource of self-examination.

Congregations are unhealthy because they go through the motions of participating in Communion ceremonies without following the process of preparation. Far too often we examine the Communion trays and cups, yet fail to examine the most important component to the celebration. Communion challenges us to fellowship with both God and each other – there must be a repentant, restored rhythm within the rite of Holy Communion. Christ died for our place at the table, and we should never take that lightly.

We must teach congregations to reflect, review, and renew each time the Communion table is set. The holy sanctified atmosphere should be so respected within the church, that people should feel a sense of reverence just seeing the table set as they enter into the sanctuary.

Communion should remind us to love the least and the lost; Communion should remind us to love God with all that is within us. Communion should remind us to love each other. It is time for the church to examine itself, and remember Christ.

Benediction

Beloved family, continue in prayer to live as Christ has led us to prosper. May the great invisible, immortal, everlasting God of peace, love, and joy make His countenance fall upon you. May He make His face to shine upon you. May the sweet guiding communion of the Holy Spirit be with you – forever!

To be continued…..

Patmos Isle Publishing
www. patmosmedia.com

Patmos Isle Publishing
www. patmosmedia.com

Patmos Isle Publishing
www. patmosmedia.com

Patmos (Πάτμος): Somewhere between 81 A.D. and 96 AD, the Apostle John was exiled to the Isle of Patmos (a rugged and bare island in the Aegean Sea); for his commitment to the word of God and testimony of Christ. John wrote the prophecy of Revelation during his island exile. *"Revelation 1:9 - I John, who also am your brother, and companion in tribulation, and in the kingdom and patience of Jesus Christ, was in the isle that is called Patmos, for the word of God, and for the testimony of Jesus Christ."*

www.ingramcontent.com/pod-product-compliance
Lightning Source LLC
Chambersburg PA
CBHW071437090426
42737CB00011B/1693